In Walks Jesus

By Peter E. Mueller

CONCORDIA PUBLISHING HOUSE • SAINT LOUIS

Edited by Rodney L. Rathmann and Thomas J. Doyle

Copyright © 1997 Concordia Publishing House
3558 South Jefferson Avenue, St. Louis, MO 63118-3968
Manufactured in the United States of America

4   5   6   7   8   9   10   11   12   13   12   11   10   09   08   07   06   05   04   03

Contents

Foreword   7

Introduction   11

Session **1**
The Skeptic   13

Session **2**
The Educated Seeker   25

Session **3**
The Social Outcast   39

Session **4**
Those Trapped in Immorality   51

Session **5**
Those in Affliction   63

Session **6**
The Grieving   75

*I gratefully acknowledge
my parents, Paul and Lyn Mueller,
for seizing everyday opportunities
in leading me to love Jesus*

Foreword

Always be ready to make your defense to anyone who demands from you an accounting for the hope that is in you. 1 Peter 3:15 NRSV

"Always be ready." Those are important words. They provide at least three important learnings. First, it is possible to be ready to share our faith. Second, you never know when the faith-sharing opportunity will arise, so readiness is the order of the day. Third, people need help and encouragement in that readiness.

This book is meant to be a tool for the Christian's readiness. It gives wise and practical steps for the Christian to take. You will find your time spent pondering and applying its points very productive in your own witness to Jesus Christ. All of us are called upon to be witnesses for Jesus Christ. 1 Peter 2:8–10 says all Christians are priests called to declare the mighty works of God. Acts 1:8 calls God's people witnesses. It is our duty and delight.

Congregations are finding that evangelism is not a program; though programmatic emphases can assist evangelism. Evangelism is not an event; though certain events can assist members in sharing their faith. Evangelism is a lifestyle. George Barna, head of Barna Research Group and an astute watcher of the churched and unchurched scene in America, writes that evangelistic congregations have this characteristic: "Their definition of success in evangelism is that people active in the church are intentionally and obediently sharing their faith with nonbelievers" (*Evangelism That Works*" page 92). In other words, evangelism is sharing Christ in the daily life of the believer. It is a lifestyle.

Yet there is need for congregations to be more intentional about the task of helping their members "always be prepared." According to the Barna Research Group, only 12 percent of pastors could say their parishioners are effectively prepared to witness; 85 percent of the Christians who actively witness said they would like to be better trained in evangelism. This book can be a valuable resource in that training.

A Partnership

This book represents a partnership between Concordia Publishing House and the Department of Evangelism Ministry of the Board for Congregational Services. Our goal is to work together to supply congregations and individuals with timely, effective, and faithful resources for training in evangelism. This book is one in a series in which the two entities are cooperating.

How to Use this Book

It is hoped that this book will be helpful in a variety of settings.

A weekly Bible class could take a number of weeks and work through this course. The text could be read ahead of time, reviewed in class, and the discussion questions could guide the class discussion.

A small group/home group could study this book over a period of meetings. This would be an excellent setting in which to take the time to encourage one another and support one another as participants take practical steps to witness to Christ.

Two Christian friends could covenant to study this book together. They could help and encourage each other. Perhaps, most important, they could hold one another accountable to the learning and doing involved in this class.

Also, an individual could read, study, ponder, and apply that which is discussed in this book by herself or himself.

Congregations working hard at equipping their members for evangelism will find many more ways to use this book.

Words of Appreciation

What a joy it has been to work with CPH and Peter Mueller on this project. We commend them for work well done. A special thanks to Peter for the fine work he did in writing these chapters. They reflect discussions from a daylong meeting and add creativity and personal touches to the notes of that day. Also, thanks to the editors at CPH for the work they have done and are doing in bringing this evangelism series into being.

It is our prayer that many will be blessed by their time in this book. Above all, we pray that all of us will grow in bold witness to our wonderful Savior, that many would come to trust His grace and that all glory will go to Him.

Rev. Jerry M. Kosberg, *Director*
Department of Evangelism Ministry
Board for Congregational Services
The Lutheran Church—Missouri Synod

Introduction

Common Encounters

I like the simple things in life. The common things. Gravel roads and burning charcoal and sky and water and distant hills. Yet I live a paradox. For although my existence is common, my beliefs are quite uncommon. I believe, for instance, in the Incarnation. I believe that God would allow Himself to be moved, out of love for the lost, to exchange His throne for a dusty pair of sandals and a walking stick.

Jesus. It staggers me to think that God would stoop to be so common. That He would take on muscle and tendon and walk among people like me. Yet "The Word became flesh and made His dwelling among us" (John 1:14). I am amazed that He would risk so much as to leave heaven for earth so that He might in turn welcome us to heaven.

Jesus didn't travel the easy road. Instead, He stepped from the throne onto the rocky Judean trails, stopping at houses and cisterns along the way to share His Father's love with the people He encountered. It has sometimes been said that doing the work of ministry would be great if it weren't for the people. Yet Jesus dealt with them not only in highly visible speaking engagements but also in obscure moments. And in all of His importance He engaged them one at a time. He walked into their towns and their homes. He strode into their conversations and their lives.

It seems that it would have been easier for Jesus to give one great sermon, Pentecost-style, and bring everyone to repentance and faith at once. Then He could have cut back on His demanding preaching schedule and spent afternoons fishing with the disciples. But He had a different type of fishing in mind. He chose to win us over one by one, coming to each of us where we are. He walked into the world of the skeptic and the seeker. He reached out to the outcast and the immoral, the afflicted and the grieving.

He spent His time with common people. People like the ones who surround me. People like me.

Common encounters. Life is filled with them. Yet most of us stumble through these everyday opportunities without taking advantage of the eternal moment. I believe there is a window in each of these encounters that holds a view of the Father, and it is my privilege to point out the view. Salvation stands waiting behind every conversation, every encounter. What an opportunity. What a challenge. What a gift.

Session 1
The Skeptic

P hilip found Nathanael and told him, "We have found the one Moses wrote about in the Law, and about whom the prophets also wrote—Jesus of Nazareth, the son of Joseph." "Nazareth! Can anything good come from there?" Nathanael asked. (John 1:45–46)

In Walks Jesus

A breeze at last. I push the window open farther, allowing a rustle of summer air to stir through the room. The room is dark, save for the warm halo thrown by the desk lamp onto the book lying open below it. All around this leather-bound volume, papers and books and green plants and photographs wrestle for a sure place on the small desk, elbowing for a chance at center stage. Yet the spotlight falls onto the text of Scripture, lying open to the Gospel of John. I return to the desk and pick up the book. I smell the leather and hear the rustle of pages. I thumb through the life recorded by John.

Page after page, Jesus moves from one place to another, from one person to the next. Chapter after chapter, what John records in detail are the *conversations* of Jesus. We see people who are going about the business of their everyday lives. Doing what they did the day before, and the day before that. Taking care of daily chores, going to weddings and funerals. And then, in walks Jesus. Their lives are never the same, nor are the lives of those who surround them. For once they have come face to face with Jesus, they have also come to see the heart of the one who sent Him. They are like the woman who encountered Jesus while she was drawing water, who raced back to her town to say, "Come, see a man who told me everything I ever did" (John 4:29).

And the text goes on to say that many of the people from that town came to believe in Him because of her testimony:

"They said to the woman, 'We no longer believe just because of what you said; now we have heard for ourselves, and we know that this man really is the Savior of the world' " (John 4:42).

Common conversations. The Gospel of John is filled with them. My life, too, is filled with conversations such as these. I talk to a woman sitting next to me on the airplane about a book she is reading. A college student strikes up a conversation with me while sitting at the coffee shop. The neighbor in the house across the street asks me a question about my church.

Common conversations frequently lead to uncommon encounters. God works faith as He wills. Yet far too often, Christians sell themselves short. When they find themselves in everyday conversations, they shy away from the thought that they could make a difference in the other person's life. They ramble on about the insignificant, shielding themselves, ironically, from speaking about what is most important to them. Their faith falters at the prospect that this conversation could be filled with eternal significance. They might be tempted to think that talking about Jesus is best left to preachers and evangelism committees. They have become content to live their eternal moments within the doors of their own church. In effect, their attitude has become similar to the one displayed in the old prayer:

God bless me and my wife,
My son John and his wife,
Us four and no more.

Christians are certainly not against the spread of the Gospel. Yet we often unknowingly become stubborn clay in the hands of the Potter. Fear and inadequacy rob us of opportunities to reach those whom God has put around us. Lack of courage keeps us from seizing the moment before us. We forget God's words to Joshua, "Have I not commanded you? Be strong and courageous. Do not be terrified; do not be discouraged, for the LORD your God will be with you wherever you go" (Joshua 1:9).

So, with the attitude of an average warrior who knows he is flanked by a superior army, I return to the pages of John. Through the urging of the Holy Spirit, I have become determined to serve as a Christian witness in my neighborhood, in my family, at work … But I need help. I feel inadequate to take on that which lies before me. I stand ready for battle but look down in embarrassment to see that I have forgotten my armor.

I consider Jesus. How did He do it? How did He just step into the life of the woman who was supposed to be His adversary by blood? What did He say to the friends and family of the man whose body had just been sealed up in the grave? How did He get through to the woman who was sleeping with a man who was not her husband?

It becomes apparent that Jesus was continually looking for common encounters through which He could point ordinary people to the Father. And where else but in the Gospel of John can we find such a detailed account of His everyday conversations? Yet as we leaf through the pages of John's account, we also gain sight of the bigger picture. Jesus is more than example. Much more. He is Savior, our Friend, the Object of our faith, and the only Path to God. John clearly tells us why he writes his account of Jesus, "But these are written that you may believe that Jesus is the Christ, the Son of God, and that by believing you may have life in His name" (John 20:31). And Jesus Himself boldly declares, "I am the way and the truth and the life. No one comes to the Father except through Me" (John 14:6).

So as we trace the prints of His sandals down the dusty trails, resting at cisterns and towns along the way, we whisper a prayer to the Father. We thank Him not only for One whom we can follow on the road but also for One who picks us up and carries us on the journey.

A Little Like Philip

I ponder the account from John, Chapter 1. The Word takes on flesh. The Baptizer cries out in the desert. Jesus begins to gather disciples. He finds a man named Philip and says, "Follow Me" (John 1:43). And in reading this account, it strikes me that I am a little like Philip.

Jesus has sought Philip out. John indicates no reason why Philip would be chosen. No exemplary character accounts, no attendance records from the synagogue. Jesus simply has gone to find him. And having found him, He has said to him, "Follow Me." The text doesn't indicate that there was any decision to be made. This disciple-in-the-making just obeyed.

Now I see Philip running up the rock-strewn road to Nathanael. Philip is wide-eyed, his breath comes in gulps. Words tumble over one another. "We have found the one Moses wrote about in the Law, and about whom the prophets also wrote" (John 1:45).

That's me. Excited and amazed and full of energy. Too-good-to-be-true and can't-wait-to-tell-you and centuries of prophecy and prayer leading up to this one moment. This one eternal moment. Almost wondering myself whether this could really be the one.

And yet I don't shout the message from the hilltops, hoping someone will listen. I don't fling out the message of the Messiah into the wind. Rather, I am more inclined to speak the message to people, one on one. People at the grocery store or the gas station. People who live across the street and around the corner.

As I turn the pages of the Holy Book, I pray that you, too, are like Philip. You have found Jesus. Or rather, He has found you. He has come after you, and having found you, has said, "Follow Me." And you have become convinced by the Spirit that this Jesus is the Christ, the one sent by God to bring us back into a right relationship with Him, by means of a stained cross and an empty grave. The one about whom Moses and the prophets spoke. And you are now out of breath, words tumbling over each other, running back to find the ones you know to tell them about this Jesus.

And so Philip found Nathanael. He has told him about the Messiah. I picture Nathanael now listening intently. But Philip continues, getting more specific in his report: "It's Jesus of Nazareth. The son of Joseph!"

This is too much. Philip has just thrown in too many details. He may as well have said, "It's the kid from around the corner, the one who was never any good at soccer." The Messiah was to have been a king. Royal blood. From Jerusalem, maybe. From the little town of Nazareth, never. Blue collar family, not on your life. The skeptic in Nathanael steps forward, and he blurts out, "Can anything good come from Nazareth?"

I wonder if Philip was prepared for the reaction he got. I wonder, if he had known what Nathanael would say, whether he might have maybe casually slid the story in over lunch. Or whether he would have first asked a few probing questions to figure out if Nathanael would be receptive to the Messiah coming from Nazareth. Or perhaps he would have remained silent about the whole thing, afraid of being laughed at.

If I had been in Philip's place, I would have responded differently to Nathanael's blunt reaction. I probably would have said, "Hey, I'll see you later, Nathanael. Forget I brought it up." Then I would have sulked off to consider whether my friendship with Nathanael was really worth having.

Philip's response, however, served to open a door rather than close one. "Nazareth! Can anything good come from there?" Nathanael had asked incredulously. And in reply, Philip said, "Come and see."

I believe that this is one of the most powerful statements in Scripture. Philip didn't worry about dealing with his skeptical friend or maneuver to protect his own ego. He merely pointed Nathanael to Jesus. *Come and see.*

And with those words, in walks Jesus.

The World of the Skeptic

Nathanael was certainly not the first skeptic of the truth that God has revealed through Jesus of Nazareth. Nor is he the last skeptic this world has seen. Even in the tapestry of John's gospel, skepticism is woven in with the clear thread of salvation. Notice some of the reactions to God's Messiah:

After He healed a blind man, the religious leaders said of Jesus: "This man is not from God, for He does not keep the Sabbath" (John 9:16).

After He spoke with a group of Jews outside the temple in Jerusalem, they took up stones and explained: "We are not stoning You for any of these [miracles] … but for blasphemy, because You, a mere man, claim to be God" (John 10:33).

And even while Jesus was dying on the cross, the chief priests of the Jews protested to Pilate: "Do not write 'The King of the Jews,' but that this man claimed to be king of the Jews" (John 19:21).

Add to this Mary's amazement that the risen Lord could be anything other than the gardener, along with Thomas' bold skepticism: "Unless I see the nail marks in His hands and put my finger where the nails were, and put my hands into His side, I will not believe it" (John 20:25). Yet God's Spirit broke through obstacles such as these to form a faith and a people who would turn the world upside down.

Reluctance to believe in Jesus of Nazareth did not die with the end of the Gospel accounts. It was not long after the events of Jesus' death and resurrection that some skeptics began in earnest to make themselves heard concerning this new religion. A pagan named Celsus was among the first to take up the pen against Christianity. His words have remarkably been preserved through the centuries:

> If these men worshiped no other God but one, perhaps they would have a valid argument against the others. But in fact they worship to an extravagant degree this man who appeared recently, and yet think it is not inconsistent with monotheism if they also worship his servant. (Frances Young, *The Making of the Creeds,* Trinity Press International © 1991 by Frances M. Young)

According to Celsus, these Christians have said too much. They have thrown in too many details. They say they worship one God. That's fine. But Celsus cannot understand how they worship both the Father and this Jesus, yet still claim to have belief in *one* God. Inconceivable.

The skepticism continues right up until today. In fact, the modern world has become a well-fertilized garden for those who doubt and distrust. Here in the United States, ever-advancing technologies and a staggering rate of change lead to loose footing. The media throws a blanket of cynicism over the attitudes of the nation. We have been trained to be skeptical of politicians and popes. We do well to become alarmed that we are raising an entire generation whose main characteristics are pessimism, disinterest, and a critical eye towards the lifestyles and beliefs of those who have gone before. We are making way for America's 13th generation (also known as the "Baby Busters," or "Generation X"), those born roughly between 1961 and 1981. Many church leaders are already beginning to carry a burden for these young skeptics. They are intentionally working to reach out with the endearing love of the Father to the people of this generation.

How do we come to understand them? William Strauss and Neil Howe, in *Thirteenth Gen: Abort, Retry, Ignore, Fail?* (New York: Random House, 1993), which chronicles their exhaustive research on the "13th Gen," describe the typical belief system of a "13er":

> In her despiritualized life, she strips billowy questions down to their real-world fundamentals. Having come of age without war but with an obsessive fear of nuclear holocaust, she sees apocalypse for what it is—just death. She sees herself as post-ideological, in some ways even post-religious. She's hesitant to impose her beliefs (on everything from school prayer to

abortion) on others. Her ... God is straightforward, prone to action. What God sells, He services; when He bills, He collects —then it's over.

Yes! It would take a miracle for anyone in our sophisticated, contemporary world to believe in a good and gracious God. It would be sheer lunacy for an upwardly mobile American to put aside his university training long enough to consider a God who "made Himself nothing, taking the very nature of a servant, being made in human likeness" (Philippians 2:7). Only the desperate would hang their hopes on a God who claims to give, while living in a world that only seems to take.

God has sent me to share my faith in such a world. He has asked me to point such a world to the Christ of the cross. But I am not alone. As God spoke to Joshua before He sent him into battle,

"No one will be able to stand up against you all the days of your life. As I was with Moses, so I will be with you; I will never leave you nor forsake you" (Joshua 1:5).

And these are the very words that Jesus echoed when He sent out His disciples.

Come and See

It would be easy for those of us who are Christians to dismiss the skeptics of this world. We could view them as unreachable or consider them to be opponents to everything that we stand for. The challenges of reaching (let alone *understanding*) the 13th Generation and other skeptics can send us scurrying for the security of our pews and paraments. The many different cultures which now surround us bring us into contact with world-views which may seem to threaten us. Yet those who verbalize their questions in response to our message are rarely hardened atheists. And we are called to bring Christ to all people.

Above all, we must remember that it is only by God's grace that any one of us has come to believe in Him. Only by grace are we able to live a life of Christian witness in this world. We are all beggars. Centuries ago, in 1537, Martin Luther pointed out the importance of this understanding, as he preached on the account of Philip and Nathanael. His words hold true, not only in his culture, but also in ours. He spoke the following words from the pulpit of the parish church in Wittenberg:

> Christ ... wants it clearly and definitely understood that all who seek entry into His kingdom must seek it by nothing but grace. Christ has regard for no one because of his pile of guldens, his beauty, his wisdom, his golden hair, or because he wears a garment embroidered in gold or silver, or a gray coat. No, it is grace alone that counts. His is to be a kingdom of grace, belonging to those who are wretched and poor, whether they be men or women, rich or poor. (*Luther's Works* 22:190–91)

We are ambassadors of the kingdom of grace. The skeptic is not our enemy. In many instances, the skeptic is no more than an outspoken seeker. We might define those who react to our message with ideas and questions as "skeptics." They might define themselves as "honest." Or "confused." Or "searching."

Notice how Jesus dealt with Nathanael's apparent skepticism. As He saw Nathanael approaching, He said, "Here is a true Israelite, in whom there is nothing false." Considering the circumstances, this was a remarkable reaction. I would have expected harsh words condemning Nathanael's unbelief. Judgment, with a possible thunderbolt. Nathanael had openly scorned God's plan. And yet Jesus warmly announced, "Here is a man who tells it like it is!" He saw Nathanael as being honest about his questions.

There are several things that we can learn from this account of Philip and Nathanael, as we prepare to deal with those who seem to be skeptical towards the Christian faith. First, we can't let rejection faze us. If Philip had let Nathanael's question discourage him, or if he had seen it as an attack, the story would have ended there. But Philip was real enough to know that Nathanael's questions were legitimate. In the same way, we must see questions to our Christian witness as being valid. We must deal with them respectfully and honestly, without letting them discourage us.

Second, our words to those who are honest about their questions need to be the same as Philip's words. "Come and see," he said. He pointed Nathanael to Jesus. He didn't try to argue him into the Kingdom. And, if you notice, the next line in John's account describes Nathanael approaching Jesus. Obviously, he had accepted Philip's invitation. He was coming to Jesus to see for himself.

In his book *Dare to Be Different* (Concordia Publishing House, 1997), Stephen Hower describes the importance of this second step:

Conversion does not rest on a Christian's ability to articulate an air-tight presentation. That is a no-win approach to witnessing, because when you win by argumentation you still lose. And when you lose by argumentation you also lose. As the old axiom correctly states, Those convinced against their will remain unconvinced. Conversion is God's business, not ours.

Dealing with rejection and confidently pointing the skeptic to Jesus provide the working foundation for our witness. But in the third place, we can openly affirm the skeptic's search for truth. We can applaud him for his honesty. This is what Jesus did as Nathanael approached Him. He praised his resistance to gullibility: "Here is a true Israelite, in whom there is nothing false!" Robert Kinast, an author with a keen interest in theological reflection, may help us to think through Nathanael's encounter with Jesus:

> Nathanael heard the compliment in Jesus' greeting, an implicit affirmation that the expectation of the Messiah was too important to be bestowed on every fresh preacher in the valley. Claims had to be examined, impressions had to be tested, truth had to prevail ... Jesus was up to the challenge. "Before Philip called you, I saw you under the fig tree" (1:48).
>
> (From *If you Only Recognized God's Gift*, copyright © 1993 by Wm. B. Eerdmans Publishing Co. Used by permission.)

Jesus was already beginning to answer Nathanael's questions. In fact, He was answering questions that Nathanael hadn't even formed in his own mind yet. This leads us into our fourth point. For we must understand that Jesus had His eye on Nathanael long before Nathanael came to see Jesus. Nathanael was amazed that Jesus was aware of him and asked incredulously, "How do You know me?" (John 1:48).

I have a friend who currently attends a state university. Through his study of philosophy, he has come to believe that religion has been cooked up in man's mind. He now thinks that "God" is a development of man's desire to have something in life which is greater than himself. Concepts of God flow from a need to order and understand the world.

There are many who would agree with my friend. Yet an amazing reversal takes place when one realizes that "God" is not a product of man, but that man is a product of God. God does not dwell inside the mind, but the mind rests within God's infinite creation. And God intimately knows each part of His creation. "I saw you while you were still under the fig tree before Philip called you" (John 1:48).

The mystery of salvation is in the hands of God. Yet God's people have been given a hand in this mystery. As Paul writes to the church in Rome, "Through Him and for His name's sake, we received grace and apostleship to call people from among all the Gentiles to the obedience that comes from faith. And you also are among those who are called to belong to Jesus Christ" (Romans 1:5–6).

It is God alone who brings non-Christians to saving faith. Yet for some strange reason He chooses to use common people such as us in the process. In 2 Corinthians, Paul compares this to putting a treasure in jars of clay. He points out that "we have this treasure in jars of clay to show that this all-surpassing power is from God and not from us" (2 Corinthians 4:7).

So how do we handle this treasure that has been given us? There is an old saying which goes, Before you talk to a friend about God, talk to God about that friend. Our weaknesses, fears, and failures remind us that the power at work in our Christian witness comes "from God and not from us."

And so, finally, Nathanael is able to respond, "You are the Son of God; You are the King of Israel" (John 1:49). He has just confessed the words that stand as the goal of John's gospel ("These are written that you may believe that Jesus is the Christ, the Son of God"). This confession comes not because of Philip's persuasiveness, but because Nathanael has come face to face with the Son of God. Jesus says to him, "You believe because I told you I saw you under the fig tree." But He goes on to say, "You shall see greater things than that" (John 1:50).

Jesus, in effect, is saying, "You haven't seen anything yet!" And this is the final point that we need to remember as we consider this section from John 1. The skeptic may have an initial understanding of Christ which is incomplete. That is nothing for us to be afraid of. A confession of Christ, no matter how inadequate, is made possible only by the stirrings of the Spirit. The same questioning mind that leads the skeptic to Jesus will also lead him deeper and deeper into that relationship with Christ. And we stand ready to help him deal with his honest questions. We might bring a friend along to meet Jesus, but that is not the end of the road. It is only the beginning.

For Discussion

1. In the Introduction, the statement is made, "Salvation stands waiting behind every conversation, every encounter." Have you ever considered your contacts with people to have such potential? What factors lead you to turn down such opportunities? Tell of a time when God led you to pursue such an opportunity.

2. Why does God's Word need to be the starting point for any discussion of Christian witness? Look again at the first paragraph of this chapter. Which details here might have been included to serve as *pictures* of the power of God's Word among us (e.g., the rustle of air in the room, the halo of light, the green plants, the photographs)?

3. Do you know anyone who seems to be questioning or critical of the Christian message? How have you responded to that person in the past? Has this chapter helped you to see more clearly how you might deal with that person in the future? If so, describe your new plan of action.

4. Paul writes in Ephesians, "For it is by grace you have been saved, through faith—and this not from yourselves, it is the gift of God—not by works, so that no one can boast" (Ephesians 2:8–9). What is grace? How do the words of this passage make all the difference in the life of a Christian? Why do we need to remember these words in considering our contacts with non-Christians?

5. State, in your own words, several points which can be learned from Nathanael's experience with Philip and Jesus.

Session *2* The Educated Seeker

Now there was a man of the Pharisees named Nicodemus, a member of the Jewish ruling council. He came to Jesus ... (John 3:1–2)

Make the Most of Every Opportunity

The voice came from behind the stall in the men's room: "So what about the blasphemy against the Holy Spirit?"

I chuckled to find myself in such a significant conversation while standing in a public rest room. Yet I finished drying my hands and stood outside the stall and answered toward the metal partition in front of me. "Well, that's the one sin in the Bible that God talks about which won't be forgiven," I replied. "It's amazing to think that God will forgive any sin we could commit, except for the sin of persistently shutting out the work of the Holy Spirit. But when you think about it, you're shutting out the very One who is able to bring you to faith." And so our conversation continued.

I still shake my head and smile when I think about that conversation. I have come to recognize that God works through common encounters. But how common can you get? Shouldn't there be a certain degree of dignity to our conversations about things divine?

Then I think back to Jesus' conversations with the men that He was crucified with. Criminals. Hanging together on gore-stained trees. Mixture of sweat and spittle, buzzing flies. How much dignity could possibly be preserved in such a scene? But Jesus used the moment to invite one more into the Kingdom.

I have always loved the passage from Colossians in which Paul says, "Devote yourselves to prayer, being watchful and thankful. And pray for us, too, that God may open a door for our message, so that we may proclaim the mystery of Christ" (Colossians 4:2–3).

I remember seeing that passage for the first time when I was in the Phoenix headquarters of the relief organization, Food for the Hungry. They had printed this verse onto business cards, which were available at the front desk. The passage struck me so deeply that I picked up a card and carried it around in my wallet for the next couple of years. "Pray for us, too, that God may open a door for our message." Little did I know that the "door" Paul was speaking of would on this day be attached to the stall of a men's room. But such is the unpredictable nature of the Gospel. Such is the creative delight of a Father who loves His children.

And so I continue to look for opportunities to encounter "the eternal moment," regardless of unusual circumstances. I continue to pray for Eric, the one whom God led across my path on that particular day. It seemed like a normal trip to the bathroom. But then God began to open a door.

Eric started the conversation. Here we go, I thought. I got a talker. But he didn't talk about the St. Louis Cardinals. He didn't comment on the high humidity. He didn't share his views on the upcoming election. Instead, he brought up a question. A conversation-starter. But somehow that question led to a discussion of spiritual things.

Now, don't ask me what I did to set the right climate for this discussion. It was God's timing, not mine. But I immediately sensed that the Holy Spirit was at work in this conversation. So I silently whispered a prayer asking forgiveness for my impatience and apathy. I prayed for an opportunity. I came out of my self-absorbed world and prepared for an eternal encounter.

I discovered quickly that this young man was well-schooled in matters of religion. He had been raised in a Roman Catholic church and had attended a Catholic school, although he was not currently involved in any church. He was familiar with fairly advanced Christian teachings. (How many people have questioned you lately about the biblical doctrine of sinning against the Holy Spirit?) He showed interest in life and death, in God and the church. Yet he had a lot of questions. His cousin had died recently and that had started him thinking. In fact, it had been troubling him. His cousin was only 43 when he died, and Eric had attended the funeral at an evangelical Christian church. The pastor there had said some things during the funeral service which made him think. He was thinking still.

"I've got a lot of questions," he said again.

We talked some more, but our conversation had to end all too soon. "My name's Eric," he said. "I'm Pete," I said. We shook hands. "Keep asking questions," I said as he walked out of the room. And, uncannily, it was only a couple of hours later that I ran into him again (thankfully, with a change of location). "Hey, Pete," he said, as if we had grown up together. "Hey, Eric," I said. And so the conversation continued where it had left off.

I would call Eric an educated seeker. He would probably call himself confused. He has a lot of information, but he hasn't quite made sense of it all. His mind continues to probe, to question, to poke at the Infinite. I'm not sure where Eric is today. And I'm not sure if he has saving faith or not. But God hasn't asked me to pick out the saved from the unsaved. That's His job, not mine. He has simply told me to be faithful. He has asked me to stand as a clear witness to the person and work of Jesus Christ. St. Paul wrote, as inspired by the Holy Spirit, in the letter to the Colossians, "Be wise in the way you act toward outsiders; make the most of every opportunity. Let your conversation be always full of grace, seasoned with salt, so that you may know how to answer everyone" (Colossians 4:5–6).

A Seeker Harvest

Eric is not the only one who is searching for the truth. People like Eric walk in and out of our lives each day. Even the Christian churches in our country have come to acknowledge "seekers" as a group to be targeted within our communities. "Seeker services" are advertised openly by Christian congregations in hopes of attracting the unchurched. A search for the spiritual seems to have taken on a new urgency. The next time you walk through the mall, look for items which have spiritual themes. Calendars on the Psalms. Angels everywhere. Countless books on spirituality, providing valuable advice on how to work toward inner peace. Hallmark creates and displays cards with comforting messages from a God that anyone could come to like.

Newsweek and network television probe the biblical book of Genesis, sparking new studies and old spats. Headlines, too, carry religious themes: "Hollywood Looks to Divine for Inspiration."

Ah, Hollywood. The movie industry has always dabbled in religious themes. But the full-length biblical epics of a generation ago have given way to movies about angels and energies.

The teens and young adults of today are struggling to synthesize a religion which makes sense to them. But they are the first generation in America's history which is not using Christianity as a starting point. Instead, the majority of this group is creating a belief system based on secularism, New Age, and Buddhism. Throw in a little Catholicism and Mormonism. It's like walking down a 40-foot salad bar, creating an individual salad to suit your appetite, whatever that might be. A little of this, a dab of that. Add some Protestantism for dressing and sprinkle a few Islam croutons on top. Call this concoction Christianity, because we're a Christian nation, right? It makes sense and all hangs together pretty well. But it's a far cry from biblical Christianity.

At first glance, we might become discouraged. But take a closer look at the world around you. Think then of Jesus' words to His disciples:

> I tell you, open your eyes and look at the fields! They are ripe for harvest. Even now the reaper draws his wages, even now he harvests the crop for eternal life, so that the sower and the reaper may be glad together. Thus the saying 'One sows and another reaps' is true. I sent you to reap what you have not worked for. Others have done the hard work, and you have reaped the benefits of their labor." (John 4:35b–38)

We have an incredible opportunity before us. God is sending out the workers to gather in the harvest even as you read these words. Consider, for example, those who are creating their own religion. Although they are starting from a non-Christian base, the important thing is that they are *interested* in spiritual things. Thank God they are searching! Yet we must remember that the harvest doesn't just happen. In 6,000 years, I don't believe a field ever harvested itself and put itself into barns. The present harvest involves us more intimately than we would sometimes like to acknowledge. There is no automated farm machinery in this scenario. Remember how in Matthew's gospel, Jesus talked to His disciples about this very thing. He said,

"The harvest is plentiful but the workers are few. Ask the Lord of the harvest, therefore, to send out workers into His harvest field" (Matthew 9:37b–38).

And Jesus' very next action was to send *them* out. They were to communicate the message, "The kingdom of heaven is near," both through what they said and by what they did (Matthew 10).

Relating to a message about a "harvest" can be difficult for those of us who have grown up within a half-mile of two gas stations and a Taco Bell. But God provides teachable moments for each of us. He leads us into situations where He can bring the eternal Word to life.

Willing Workers?

So, how can I get a handle on this? How does God prepare the workers for the harvest? How does He bring us to the point where we willingly step out into the fields? I believe that He starts at the cross of Calvary. God has given up everything for the sake of those whom He loves. The King cancels the enormous debt the servants owe Him (see Matthew 18:23–34). He writes the letters P-A-I-D across the details of our ledger sheet, not with black ink, but with scarlet red letters, sprawled out in blood. The blood of His own Son. We read in 1 Peter 3:18,

"For Christ died for sins once for all, the righteous for the unrighteous, to bring you to God."

The unrighteous have nothing to offer. They merely receive the gift from the Righteous One. Any understanding of our actions to reach the seeker must, therefore, begin at the cross. Our lives are lived in gratitude to the King. But it is easy to grow numb to this reality over a period of time. Life on earth seems so far removed from the reality of Calvary. Images of God on the throne being worshiped by thousands upon thousands become blurry as we channel-surf through CNN, MTV, and ESPN. But God is on the throne. And He continually uses everyday events to work out the impact of this truth in the lives of His people.

In my own life, I think back to a weekend mission trip that I took to Mexico a couple of years ago. God used the relationships and activities which took place over three days to help me walk past my own self-absorption and into the waiting fields.

A group from our church had been organized to help out in the little town of Imuris for a couple of days. Before we piled into vans for the trek across the border, each of the 30 participants was asked to memorize the hymn, "Lord of the Living Harvest." This rote memorization seemed a waste of time when we first began, but it was part of our covenant together—one element of our spiritual journey. Our physical journey involved constructing buildings and spending time with 60 little children who lived together in an *orfanatorio*.

As God would have it, the words of that hymn worked their way through our lives as we spent the next days together. They were behind our determined eyes as we mixed load after load of cement in wheelbarrows, using shovels and hoes. They were behind our smiles as we competed with seven-year-olds to balance on 50-gallon barrels. The words came up from our throats as we worshiped God together with our new friends. By the time the trip was over, those words meant more to us than I can describe on this page. I will never again see God's words about "the harvest" in the same way.

I would encourage you to ponder these words for a while. Then pray them to the Lord of the Harvest, asking Him to use you in the eternally significant work that stands before us:

> Lord of the living harvest
> That whitens on the plain,
> Where angels soon shall gather
> Their sheaves of golden grain,
> Accept these hands to labor,
> These hearts to trust and love,
> And with them ever hasten
> Your kingdom from above.
>
> As laborers in Your vineyard,
> Help them be ever true,
> Content to bear the burden
> Of weary days for You,
> To ask no other wages
> When You will call them home
> Than to have shared the labor
> That makes Your kingdom come.
>
> Be with them, God the Father,
> Be with them, God the Son
> And God the Holy Spirit,
> Most blessed Three in One.
> Teach them, as faithful servants
> You rightly to adore,
> And fill them with Your fullness
> Both now and evermore.

Equipment for Bringing in the Harvest

We are indeed surrounded by a waiting harvest. There is no need to travel to foreign countries to share the message of Jesus Christ. God has sown the fields so that they stand right outside our front doors. The richest soil is ironically found at the curbs of our cities. The harvest is waiting across the street and around the corner. When your neighbor says, "What church do you attend?" go back to your garage and get your sickle. When your co-worker asks, "How do you deal with the ups and downs of life so well?" get ready to bind up the shafts into bundles.

Yet we all know it's not that easy. What do we say when a comment from a seeker gives us a hint of the waiting harvest? It's not as simple as pulling out a scythe or rake. It's difficult sometimes to know how to respond.

It may help us to remember an account from the gospel of John, the third chapter. For here we come to realize that "educated seekers" are not merely a phenomenon of our technological world. Seekers have been around for a long time:

"Now there was a man of the Pharisees named Nicodemus, a member of the Jewish ruling council. He came to Jesus at night" (John 3:1–2).

We should note a couple of things before we move on. Here was a man who ranked, first of all, among the Pharisees. That will prove to be a significant detail in understanding Nicodemus' actions. You see, the Pharisees had a passionate devotion to the law of God. They felt they were specially called to holiness. They spent their whole lives studying, applying, and keeping (albeit, hypocritically) the Law. Under the Roman administration the Pharisees were represented in the Sanhedrin, although they were in a minority. New Testament scholar F. F. Bruce provides the following insight on the Pharisees:

> Because of their meticulous concern for the laws of purity and tithing, they could not associate easily with those, even among their fellow-Jews, who were not so particular in this regard as they themselves were. (*Paul, An Apostle of the Heart Set Free*, Copyright © 1977 The Paternoster Press Ltd.)

Yet John records that Nicodemus, a Pharisee and also a member of the Sanhedrin, came to Jesus! Just a few verses before this, in chapter 2, Jesus had cleared the temple of those who had turned His Father's house into a market. The conflict with the Jews had already begun and would escalate until it had led Jesus all the way to His execution. Notice the clash of worlds already beginning, as people responded to His bold act in the temple: "Then the Jews demanded of Him, 'What miraculous sign can You show us to prove Your authority to do all this?'" (John 2:18).

Contact with Jesus was not desirable for any Pharisee at this point. It goes without saying that the Sanhedrin would not be inviting Jesus to speak at their next luncheon. Yet Nicodemus ventures out at night to meet with Him.

I wonder how many evenings Nicodemus stewed over this decision before he actually worked up the nerve to go? What intrigued him so much about this man from Galilee? Was the meeting worth the risks involved?

Nicodemus indeed risked everything by going to Jesus. Nicodemus was a man of the Pharisees. He was a member of the Jewish ruling council. Everything he had learned and everything he stood for was in danger of being turned upside down. If John had recorded his gospel in our day, he probably would have entitled this section, "Nicodemus Encounters A Paradigm Shift." For in the conversation that follows, we see that Jesus did not uphold the keeping of the Law as the ticket to the kingdom of heaven. Rather, He placed an unsettling emphasis on water, wind, light, and spirit. God's kingdom cannot be entered by keeping rules but by keeping faith in one who loved the world so much that "He gave His one and only Son, that whoever believes in Him shall not perish but have eternal life" (John 3:16).

Nicodemus was driven by a desire to know the truth. He saw something at work in the person of Jesus Christ, and he had to find out more. Regardless of his investment in the existing religious paradigm, this first-century seeker went to see someone whom he thought would have some answers. And so he opened the conversation: "Rabbi, we know You are a teacher who has come from God. For no one could perform the miraculous signs You are doing if God were not with Him" (John 3:2).

Nicodemus had not yet acknowledged Jesus to be God, nor to be God's Messiah. Yet he had come to recognize the hand of God in Jesus' life. We, too, will attract others who do not yet know that Jesus is the Christ. There will be those who see the hand of

God in our lives and desire to know more about the faith that we hold. Recall the words that Peter wrote to a group of Christians centuries ago: "Finally, all of you, live in harmony with one another; be sympathetic, love as brothers, be compassionate and humble. Do not repay evil with evil or insult with insult, but with blessing, because to this you were called. … Always be prepared to give an answer to everyone who asks you to give the reason for the hope that you have. But do this with gentleness and respect" (1 Peter 3:8–9, 15).

Notice, in this section of Scripture, how the Christian life precedes the Christian witness. Actions, then words. It has been said frequently that Christians need to be "Jesus with skin on" in this world. Yet as we interact with the seekers in our own lives, we must "always be prepared to give an answer" for the hope that we have. Nicodemus came to Jesus and began the conversation. But from there, Jesus took full advantage of the open door. He began to teach.

The Teachable Moment

Have you ever found yourself talking when no one was listening? For a sensitive communicator, this can prove to be a terrifying experience. For some preachers, this is a weekly occurrence. We would be wise to look closely at Jesus' example in the gospels. He talked when people were ready to listen. He taught when people were ready to learn. In fact, His teaching was repeated, memorized, distributed by word of mouth, and eventually recorded with pen and ink.

What made Jesus such a great communicator? I believe that Jesus taught so effectively by relying on the use of the *question*. Notice how often He taught in response to a question that an individual posed to Him. And if there wasn't a question at hand, notice how Jesus asked a question of His own. Notice how He told stories to *create* a question for His hearers. Through His use of questions, Jesus created teachable moments. Jesus knew that when people had questions, they were ready for answers.

So in true form as a communicator of God's plan, Jesus traded answers for questions in His conversation with Nicodemus. He created a series of puzzles in the mind of this Pharisee. Nicodemus had begun the conversation with a comment. But notice how Nicodemus contributed to the rest of the conversation. Following his open-ing line, his share of the dialog consisted only of two questions and one incredulous remark: " 'How can a man be born when he is old?' Nicodemus asked. 'Surely he cannot enter a second time into his mother's womb to be born!' " (John 3:4). "How can this be?" (John 3:9).

It seems like a common conversation. Questions, comments, a sharing of ideas. Yet through this conversation Jesus strove to open an eternal door in the life of this seeker. Similarly, God will use us to bring His life-changing Word to the seekers who wander in and out of our lives in their search for truth. God has, indeed, given us equipment for the harvest. We can begin by observing Jesus' exam-ple as He dealt with Nicodemus. You may want to take note of sev-eral points in dealing with the educated seeker in your own life:

1. Don't be afraid of questions. Too often we see the questions of seekers as a threat to our beliefs or to our balance. Welcome the questions of the seeker as an opportunity to teach. Questions brought Nicodemus to Jesus. Questions create seekers. Questions lead to the eternal Answer. As St. Augustine observed already in the fourth century, "Our hearts are restless, O God, until they find their rest in Thee."

2. Pray for God to act through the teachable moment. I am often comforted by considering God's promise to the exiles in Babylon, which He spoke through the prophet Jeremiah: " 'Then you will call upon Me and come and pray to Me, and I will listen to you. You will seek Me and find Me when you seek Me with all your heart. I will be found by you,' declares the Lord" (Jeremiah 29:12–14a).

The nation of Judah was to be placed in a "teachable moment" by means of exile into Babylon. They would then be ready to seek God. As you enter a conversation with a seeker, pray that the life-giving wind of God's Spirit would blow through the life of that per-son. Pray that the seeker would be moved to search out the truth as revealed by God in Jesus Christ. Commit the soul of that person, in prayer, to the care of the Father.

3. In your conversations with those who are searching out the truth, respect where they're coming from. Don't assume they are ignorant just because they have never heard of David and Goliath or the missionary journeys of Paul. Many of them have invested a life-time to reach the spiritual understandings that they presently hold. Many of them have spent years studying philosophy or theology.

Take the time to listen carefully, but then don't be afraid to speak. Start where they are starting, but don't leave them there.

4. Be firm in your presentation of God's truth. Clearly share God's plan for your friend, centered in Jesus Christ (see again John 3:16). You may be tempted to water down the Gospel in order to build a connection. Don't do it. It's a trick of the adversary. If you simply look for points that you and another can person agree on, you will probably talk a lot about "love" or "God," but rarely about Jesus. Keep winding your way back to the cross and the empty tomb! The devil will wail and moan because of it! Be aware that if you don't go to the cross, you may end up walking down the same "religious salad bar" where many seekers wander in search of spiritual nurture.

Go back to the story of Jesus and Nicodemus. Notice how Jesus held His ground when it came to the truth. He even got in Nicodemus' face at one point during the discussion: " 'You are Israel's teacher,' said Jesus, 'and you do not understand these things? I tell you the truth, we speak of what we know, and we testify to what we have seen, but still you people do not accept our testimony. I have spoken to you of earthly things and you do not believe; how then will you believe if I speak of heavenly things?' " (John 3:10–12).

You may need to "say it like it is." Just don't allow the conversation to work its way into an argument. Remember the lesson from the Crusades: killing others for the sake of Christianity might create a certain smugness in the heart of the warrior, but it wins very few converts.

5. Be loving in your presentation of God's truth. Some of Jesus' comments to Nicodemus might seem a bit abrupt to us at first. Yet throughout this conversation, He continued to expose the tender heart of God who loves all of His creation. Jesus valued Nicodemus as a person. It is obvious that He wanted Him to come to understand the truth. He clearly shared God's love for Nicodemus as He carefully took the time to teach him.

6. Look for a starting point so that you might clearly share the message of Christ crucified. In speaking with Nicodemus, Jesus repeatedly pointed to the Son (Himself) as the one way to the Father. In the same way, we need to untiringly hold Christ up as the center of our beliefs. We need to look for an "in," so that we might share the message of the cross with others.

Let's look more closely to see how Jesus found this starting point with Nicodemus. Now Jesus knew that Nicodemus was familiar with the Law. He had most likely memorized significant portions of the Old Testament. He could probably recite from memory the account of Moses casting a bronze serpent and putting it up on a pole in the desert. He was well aware of God's promise, that any Israelite might look at it and so be saved from the bites of the poisonous snakes (Numbers 21:6–9). Jesus chose this common ground as a starting point in sharing God's plan: "Just as Moses lifted up the snake in the desert, so the Son of Man must be lifted up, that everyone who believes in Him may have eternal life" (John 3:14–15).

Look for an open door. Be bold to talk about Jesus. Remember that without Christ, we are no longer Christians. Remember how Peter confidently spoke out concerning the risen Jesus, in the face of a hostile group of Jewish rulers: "Salvation is found in no one else, for there is no other name under heaven given to men by which we must be saved" (Acts 4:12).

7. Finally, don't lose sight of the fact that your conversation with a seeker is only one tile in a larger mosaic. It is one element in a continuing work of God. It's not up to you to convert the seeker. That is best left to the care of the Spirit, which, like the wind, "blows wherever it pleases" (John 3:8). Simply act as a faithful witness, one who is "always … prepared to give the reason for the hope that you have" (1 Peter 3:15).

And who knows how God will work through your willingness to "go out into the fields"? In the encounter between Jesus and Nicodemus, the conversation ends with the reader wondering if this conversation has done any good. It almost seems as though Nicodemus is beyond hope ("I have spoken to you of earthly things and you do not believe"). Yet God's story is not over. For John records two other references to Nicodemus in his gospel. In the first of these, Nicodemus speaks out among the Pharisees to defend Jesus (John 7:50–51). In the second reference, Nicodemus goes with Joseph of Arimathea to take away Jesus' body after He was crucified (John 19:39–42). Together they wrap His body, with spices, in strips of linen. Then they lay it in the tomb.

Now tell me. Does it sound as though this individual is merely an educated seeker? Or does he appear to be a disciple of Jesus Christ?

I wonder where Nicodemus is today …

For Discussion

1. Read Colossians 4:3–4 once more. Are there any events from your own life which come to mind, as you read these verses? What doors are now standing open before you, so that you might "proclaim the mystery of Christ"? Now read Colossians 4:2. As you look to future opportunities to share your faith, what habits might you form so that you intentionally ... devote yourself to prayer? are watchful? are thankful?

2. Do you agree that this is the age of the seeker? In what ways have you noticed an openness to spiritual things in the world around you?

3. "The harvest is plentiful but the workers are few. Ask the Lord of the harvest, therefore, to send out workers into His harvest field" (Matthew 9:37b–38). What reaction do you have to the thought that God is ready to send *you* out to harvest?

4. What do you think about Nicodemus? Do you respect him? Scorn him? Relate to him? With what emotions might a seeker be forced to deal when considering what he or she stand to lose and gain by becoming a believer in Jesus?

5. Which of the seven suggestions for dealing with the educated seeker was most helpful for you? Why?

Session 3 The Social Outcast

Jesus, tired as He was from the journey, sat down by the well ... When a Samaritan woman came to draw water, Jesus said to her, "Will you give Me a drink?" ... The Samaritan woman said to Him, "You are a Jew and I am a Samaritan woman. How can You ask me for a drink?" (For Jews do not associate with Samaritans.) (John 4:6-7, 9)

Cooties

I hold only a vague understanding of what it means to be an outcast. It is difficult for me to truly empathize with one who is on the outside. I have, almost without exception, experienced the security of being accepted by those around me.

While growing up, I was heckled on occasion, but rarely was it something that I couldn't handle. For instance, when I was in seventh grade, there was a period of several weeks when my size 13 shoes (showboated on a 12-year-old body) were the object of lunch-hour jeers. In sixth grade a kid used to flick my ears because they stuck out away from the side of my head. And in fifth grade a girl had asked me once if I was a "Jesus freak." But I have never experienced persistent abuse over a long period of time. I have been fortunate. In looking back to those years, however, I am still touched by a pang of guilt for the part that I played in placing (and keeping) someone *else* on the outside of the group.

It was while I attended a Christian elementary school that I became aware of the fact that some people just don't belong. Some people are not as acceptable as others. Some individuals are not entitled to the same respect and belonging that the rest of us enjoy. Some seem destined to play the role of the outcast. In my experience, this position belonged to a girl named Emily. And each year as our class moved on to the next grade, Emily went right with us as the object of our thoughtless words and actions.

The sing song phrase, "Emily's germs, no returns," will be forever embedded in my mind. I remember a regular game of playing "keep away" from Emily at recess. I picture second-grade children switching places in line so that they wouldn't have to stand by the outcast of our class. I have a memory of a third-grade boy gagging and writhing because Emily had brushed against him. I can hear the mounting chant, "You've got Emily's cooties, you've got Emily's cooties," as this little show gained crowd support. I still can see her cheeks puckering up in frustration and her eyes eventually overflowing with tears.

I think back, trying to remember what this girl did to warrant such treatment. I seem to recall that her family didn't have much money. She wasn't as bright as some of the rest of us. And maybe she wasn't always very clean. And if you had to hold her hand for prayer, you would discover that her palms were usually clammy.

Now I think back and see Emily as a child of the Father. Now I wish I could go back and deliberately stand by her for prayer, just to show the others that it was okay. But at the time I participated with the class in playing by the rules, and the class rules said that she was on the outside. So that's where she stayed.

I'm sure that my grade school was not the only one in which certain individuals were placed on the outside. I'm sure that many who now read these words wish that they could go back to express compassion for the Emilys of their past. I'm certain that some of you who read this still carry the pain from playing the role Emily played. What happens in our schools, however, is merely a reflection of the divisions which are made every day on the basis of nationality, belief, beauty, or wealth. If you have witnessed the cruelty of children in school, then you have, in effect, looked out the window and into the world.

Setting the Scene

How do we bring God's love in Christ to the person who is on the outside? How do we reach someone who has been hardened through a lifetime of alienation? How do we reverse the devastating tides that have been brought into shore by the pull of hatred and exclusion?

We turn again to Jesus' example in the gospel of John. But before we can understand the drama which unfolds there, we need to set the scene. To understand Jesus' encounter with the social outcast, we need to back up from His day by approximately 800 years.

We need to place ourselves in the final days of the reign of King Hoshea, the last ruler of Israel.

In 2 Kings 17 we read that Hoshea had become king of Israel in Samaria and consequently reigned for nine years. Yet the biblical record testifies that "he did evil in the eyes of the LORD" (2 Kings 17:2). Not unusual for a king of Israel. He rejected God, just like the previous 18 kings of Israel. Notice how the story of Israel's fate now unfolds:

> "Shalmaneser king of Assyria came up to attack Hoshea, who had been Shalmaneser's vassal and had paid him tribute. But the king of Assyria discovered that Hoshea was a traitor. ... The king of Assyria invaded the entire land, marched against Samaria and laid siege to it for three years. In the ninth year of Hoshea, the king of Assyria captured Samaria and deported the Israelites to Assyria. He settled them in Halah, in Gozan on the Habor River and in the towns of the Medes" (2 Kings 17:3-6).

Why would God forsake Israel? Why would He allow this to happen to His chosen people? The text answers our questions as it continues:

> "All this took place because the Israelites had sinned against the LORD their God, who had brought them up out of Egypt from under the power of Pharaoh king of Egypt. They worshiped other gods and followed the practices of the nations the LORD had driven out before them, as well as the practices that the kings of Israel had introduced. ... The Israelites persisted in all the sins of Jeroboam and did not turn away from them until the LORD removed them from His presence, as He had warned through all His servants the prophets. So the people of Israel were taken from their homeland into exile in Assyria, and they are still there" (2 Kings 17:7-8, 22-23).

The Assyrians were dreaded in their day. The successful expansion of the Assyrian empire was guaranteed through many of the tactics that they employed. One such tactic was to obliterate entire races of people from the conquered areas. This was done by exporting the people who lived there and importing others to take their place. Assyria's ruthless dealings with Israel were by the book: "The king of Assyria brought people from Babylon, Cuthah, Avva, Hamath and Sepharvaim and settled them in the towns of Samaria to replace the Israelites. They took over Samaria and lived in its towns" (2 Kings 17:24).

Over time, these foreigners intermarried with the Israelites who remained. As the years went by and new generations were born, this group of people took on an identity of their own. They became known as "Samaritans." By Jesus' day, there was nothing but sharp animosity between this mixed-blood race and the Jews, who, from their own perspective, had been preserved as the true remnant of God's chosen people.

This background helps us to understand the clash between the Samaritans and Jews in the gospels. In the book of Luke, we find an account of a Samaritan town that refused to welcome Jesus, because He was on his way to Jerusalem. It was not unusual for Samaritans to be openly hostile towards Jews who were on their way to observe religious festivals in Jerusalem. Since Samaritans often denied overnight lodging to these Jewish travelers, many Jews would journey east of the Jordan river, completely avoiding Samaria, on their way from Galilee to Jerusalem. Luke records details which convey the unashamed tension between Samaritans and Jews: "As the time approached for Him to be taken up to heaven, Jesus resolutely set out for Jerusalem. And He sent messengers on ahead, who went into a Samaritan village to get things ready for Him; but the people there did not welcome Him, because He was heading for Jerusalem. When the disciples James and John saw this, they asked, 'Lord, do you want us to call down fire from heaven to destroy them?' " (Luke 9:51–54).

Things were not exactly friendly between these two races. To the Jews, the Samaritans were social outcasts at best, despised enemies at worst. And so it was even more remarkable that one day Jesus walked into the life of a Samaritan woman, being so bold as to even ask her for a drink of water.

Who's Got the Real Water?

It probably seemed like any other day. Not much happening in the dusty town of Sychar. Yet something strange happened that noon when she trudged down the familiar trail to draw water from the well just outside of town. She noticed a traveler sitting there by the well. He was alone. At a glance she saw that He was a Jew, and so she set her jaw and went about her business. She just wished He would move back from the well so she could get her work done. Sweaty Jew. Why couldn't He pick a different spot to rest before moving on?

But then the most amazing thing happened. The traveler asked her for a drink. And in God's grand scheme, social barriers were about to come tumbling down. Salvation stood waiting. This would be a day like no other.

The woman was incredulous. A Jewish teacher should never have engaged in conversation with a woman. And a Jew asking a Samaritan to share a drink of water was unthinkable. She knew the rules. She said to Him, " 'You are a Jew and I am a Samaritan woman. How can You ask me for a drink?' (For Jews do not associate with Samaritans)" (John 4:9).

Yet Jesus wasn't about to play by the rules. At least not these rules. He had a better game in mind than the one that was generally played in this region of Palestine. He said to her, "If you knew the gift of God and who it is that asks you for a drink, you would have asked Him and He would have given you living water" (John 4:10).

There He goes again. Creating puzzles in the minds of His hearers. Forming questions that will lead them into His answer. And so this Samaritan woman, like Nicodemus before her, was led deeper into a conversation of eternal consequence. Responding to the situation she saw before her, she said,

"Sir … You have nothing to draw with and the well is deep. Where can You get this living water? Are You greater than our father Jacob, who gave us the well and drank from it himself, as did also his sons and his flocks and herds?" (John 4:11–12).

Jesus had been waiting for this obvious question. And He was prepared to give His answer: "Everyone who drinks this water will be thirsty again, but whoever drinks the water I give him will never thirst. Indeed, the water I give him will become in him a spring of water welling up to eternal life" (John 4:13–14).

Please don't miss what is going on here. Up to this point, the Samaritan woman has been operating in the world of common things. Towns and trails, jars and wells, everyday chores and travelers. But Jesus has just pointed this woman past the everyday. He has just laid the last stone of a foundation which will turn this common conversation into an eternal encounter.

Notice how Jesus has operated up to this point. First of all, He has refused to let the rules of social standing limit His interactions. He has done the unexpected. He has done the unaccepted. He has crossed lines that no one should toy with. His method of dealing with her was a jaw-jarring display. This contact was a shock to her, would soon be a shock to His disciples, and would completely astound the people of the town. Yet it served to bring down walls which allowed this woman (and many people from that town) to eventually step across the boundaries and into the Kingdom.

Second, Jesus has again used an ordinary situation to lead into a conversation that will affect this woman forever. He looked for an opening and then stepped through it. He looked for the teachable moment by creating a puzzle in the mind of the woman. He then used the opportunity as an occasion to teach.

Finally, Jesus has pointed this outcast to a God who gives eternal life without discrimination: "but *whoever* drinks the water I give him will never thirst." (John 4:14, emphasis added)

These words may have sounded too good to be true. Jesus has directed the Samaritan woman toward the gift of God, which is distributed freely to those who believe. He now stands ready to lead her to the inexhaustible resources of the Father, given through the Son.

Salvation without discrimination. Perhaps this woman's children or grandchildren, years later, had the opportunity to hear the words of a man named Paul, who penned the following words of hope and healing: "You are all sons of God through faith in Christ Jesus, for all of you who were baptized into Christ have clothed yourselves with Christ. There is neither Jew nor Greek, slave nor free, male nor female, for you are all one in Christ Jesus. If you belong to Christ, then you are Abraham's seed, and heirs according to the promise" (Galatians 3:26–29).

No longer outsiders. No longer aliens. All now belong. God sings out His grand opera of inclusion to all of us. The music is sweet to our ears: "But our citizenship is in heaven. And we eagerly await a Savior from there, the Lord Jesus Christ, who, by the power that enables Him to bring everything under His control, will transform our lowly bodies so that they will be like His glorious body" (Philippians 3:20–21).

This Round Is on Me

In reading through this account of Jesus and the Samaritan woman, I have to admire how skillfully He brings her to faith. Yet it strikes me that in one sense Jesus has set this simple woman up. He has set her up, not in a mean or malicious way, but in a way that allows Him to teach her something. He has allowed her to believe that she has a grip on the situation. For this woman is on familiar ground. She's in her own country. It's her town. Her well. Her jar. It seems as though she's in a position of power. But then, just as soon as she's sure of her hold, Jesus points out to her that the pottery she's grasping is substandard. The jar she has been counting on is not adequate for the job.

It may be that Jesus has set us up, as well, as we come to this record of the social outcast in John's gospel. To illustrate, it may be helpful to ask the question, "Who are *you* in this story?"

How have you typically read the account of the woman at the well? Have you pictured yourself as the Samaritan woman? Or have you seen yourself more as one of the disciples, closely connected to Jesus, out running errands for Him? Or perhaps you have played the role of a neutral bystander.

I would guess that very few of us have envisioned our role as that of the despised Samaritan woman. And if we have never connected with this woman, then God is about to point out to us that our pottery is of no better use than that of the woman in the story.

God is about to pull a reversal with us. In fact, God does some of His most incredible work through reversals. Think about the great switches of Scripture: the last will be first and the first will be last. Rich made poor; poor made rich. Rebellious son made honored guest.

In reading this story, we have set ourselves up for a divine reversal. For it is likely that Christians—those of us who are "insiders"—have made some decisions about who's who in this account. We have made ourselves out to be the companions and buddies of Jesus. And we have placed those people outside the church in the role of the Samaritan woman. Over time, we have erected subtle boundaries such as these. We Christians have made many of those who are outside the church to be the "social outcasts" of our day.

And why shouldn't we? We are God's chosen people. Insiders. We know the words recorded in 1 Peter apply to us: "But you are a chosen people, a royal priesthood, a holy nation, a people belonging to God, that you may declare the praises of Him who called you out of darkness into His wonderful light" (1 Peter 2:9).

We chime in, "Yep, that's us," and offer a round of Christian high-fives. We develop a pious thankfulness that we don't act like the rest of the world.

Yet in doing so, an insidious cancer creeps into the body. We may recite the Great Commission, yet seldom target our local church's outreach events toward people groups other than our own. We talk about "love for our neighbor," but we whisper about the alcoholic or the unemployed while sipping hot coffee in the church's hallways. And we cringe to think that those who are homeless or homosexual might come to worship with us.

The aim of this section from 1 Peter, however, is not to congratulate pious Christians. The apostle continues with sobering words for each of us, reminding us from where God has lifted us up: "Once you were not a people, but now you are the people of God; once you had not received mercy, but now you have received mercy" (1 Peter 2:10).

God is pleased to unveil His great reversal. He makes something of nothing. He creates a people where there was none. He is merciful to the merciless. He gives gifts to those who showed up at the party without invitations.

Like the woman at the well, we discover that we have been set up. We were counting on using our actions or our position inside the church to run errands for Jesus. But then He has smiled and pointed to the crack in our jar. And as we stand here sheepishly, He tells us that He's got water He wants to give *us*. God is providing this round of drinks. And Jesus is buying.

It is, indeed, far too easy to see the people out *there* as the outcasts. Yet God has chosen to fling wide the doors so that outcasts like *me* might also come streaming in. And outcast I am. Just like the Samaritan woman, I have listened to Jesus' words as my tarnished past has been revealed. I have tried to fool Jesus with the bluster of sure words and confident smile, thinking perhaps to receive His nod of approval. Yet Jesus has seen through it all. And He has loved me. Like her, I might also say to Jesus, "Sir, give me this water" (John 4:15).

And we who are outcasts take note of the faith-filled response of the Samaritan woman. For what did she do when she figured out who Jesus was? She left her jug, which at one time had seemed so valuable, lying in the dirt next to the well. She was consumed with running back to town, telling everyone she knew, "Come, see a man who told me everything I ever did. Could this be the Christ?" (John 4:29).

The outcast of the story was now ready to be of service to God.

And she began immediately. No evangelism training courses. No how-to books by noted evangelists. She just began to tell other outcasts about Jesus. And obviously God used her willing service. The people from the town went out to see Jesus for themselves.

It's amazing how God will use anyone in His divine plan. I love the ending to the story: "Many of the Samaritans from that town believed in Him because of the woman's testimony" (John 4:39).

It is obvious that her testimony had something to do with their leap of faith. God is able to use you in a similar way. You, too, can share your personal words with others. Tell what God has done in your life. Talk about your common encounters with Jesus. Tell of the mercy that God has shown to the sinner who walks in a saint's shoes every day. Tell them *your* story. But then point them past yourself to the one who welcomes all people, just as He welcomed you: "And because of His words, many more became believers. They said to the woman, 'We no longer believe just because of what you said; now we have heard for ourselves, and we know that this man really is the Savior of the world' " (John 4:41–42).

Tell them about the water. Point them to the well. But let God do His work of giving them the water. And don't forget … this round is on Jesus.

Who Knows?

I pray that you have come to see how you might play a role in reaching those who are on the outside. And I hope to encourage you in this work. But I want you to know that you don't have to travel to Samaria to find a social outcast. God will oftentimes bring the lost and alienated to you. What God asks of you is the willingness and readiness to respond. A friend told me once, "Only those who have received mercy can be merciful … only those who have seen grace can be gracious." Pray that God gives you a merciful heart in response to the mercy He has already shown to you.

It was after worship one Sunday that God led me by the hand into a conversation with another man from my church. As we talked, this man began to share about his grown daughter. He said, "It's hard for me to talk about this … but my daughter is incarcerated. She's in prison and could really use some encouragement."

As the conversation unfolded, I assured him that I would write to his daughter. Despite the busy week that followed, I made the time to put down some of my thoughts on paper. I would like to share with you a couple of excerpts from my letter:

Dear Cheri,

This past Sunday your dad told me you could use some words of encouragement. I decided to share with you a few things on my mind. I pray that these words are helpful to you in some way. Above all, these words point to Jesus Christ ...

In Jesus' day, He was able to get through to the people who were aware of their sin. They were aware of how bad they were by society's standards, or the expectations of their family. They knew they didn't measure up. They knew they had messed up. Think about it: Jesus was able to get through to the prostitutes. And the tax collectors. And the "sinners," as the church people called them. And these were the ones who came to Jesus and said, "Teacher ..."

Cheri, I don't know where you stand in your relationship with God. But if you have been resisting the work of God in your life, I encourage you to stop struggling. Jesus loves you! He already lived that perfect life that you will never be able to accomplish. Through faith in Jesus' life and death and resurrection for you, know that God has accomplished for you something of eternal significance. "For God so loved the world that He gave His only Son, that whoever believes in Him should not perish but have eternal life" (John 3:16).

The promise is for you. And if God has led you to receive that promise and you find yourself "at rest" in your relationship with Him, then accept the comfort that His words can bring to you in living life itself ... today and tomorrow and next week and next year ... when Jesus says to you, "Come to Me ... and I will give you rest."

You are in my prayers. May God's richest blessings be with you.

Some time later I wrote to her again. Her parents told me that she appreciated the encouragement, but I never received a letter back from her. I prayed that God would use what I had done. But I periodically wondered if my letters had done any good.

A couple of weeks ago, a young woman came up to me after church and introduced herself. I had never seen her face, but I knew her name. Her name was Cheri. I immediately realized that this was the "woman at the well" whom God had placed in my own life. This was the woman to whom I had written. With tears at the outer creases of her eyes, she told me how much those letters had meant to her.

She went on to describe how she was able to share my letters with the other women in the prison. I couldn't believe it. The other women had seen my letters, too? How?

Cheri explained that when any of the women in the prison would get mail, all the others would try to find out who it was from. So when she had gotten my first letter, she read it to some of the women who asked her about it. And then, in their organized group time, it became known that she had gotten a letter of encouragement. So she was invited to share the letter with everyone who was gathered there that day. In a move that I would have never anticipated, God used my letter to bring the message of Jesus Christ to an entire community of persons separated from society.

Who knows how God will determine to use my words of witness from this point on? Who knows how He will use Cheri's testimony and friendship as He works in the lives of the other women from that prison? Maybe tonight a woman who spent time with Cheri will sit on a narrow cot in a bare room and hold a Bible in her hands. And she will smile as she ponders the words from John's gospel, because she knows they are true. True because they speak not only of biblical characters, but because they describe her own journey as a member of an outcast community: "Many of the Samaritans from that town believed in Him because of the woman's testimony. ... They said to the woman, 'We no longer believe just because of what you said; now we have heard for ourselves, and we know that this man really is the Savior of the world'" (John 4:39, 42).

For Discussion

1. Do you remember any occasions in which you helped to keep someone on the outside of the group? Was there ever a time in which *you* were placed on the "outside"? Describe the emotions that might come from being on the outside.

2. What groups in our society today fall into the category of

"Samaritans"? Do you have any regular interaction with a person who might feel like a social outcast? How have you interacted with that person up to this point?

3. From your own experience, do you agree that Christians sometimes subtly erect walls which turn non-Christians into "social outcasts"? What are some ways in which Christians are prone to this? How does God's Word in 1 Peter 2:10 serve to prevent this type of attitude?

4. Look up 1 Peter 1:17. In what way does God desire you to be an "outcast"? How is this a positive thing?

5. Discuss the statement, "Only those who have received mercy can be merciful ... only those who have seen grace can be gracious." How does this apply to your interactions with a social outcast? What are some suggestions that the author provides for dealing with the "social outcast" in your life?

Session 4 Those Trapped in Immorality

At dawn He appeared again in the temple courts, where all the people gathered around Him, and He sat down to teach them. The teachers of the law and the Pharisees brought in a woman caught in adultery. They made her stand before the group and said to Jesus, "Teacher, this woman was caught in the act of adultery. In the Law Moses commanded us to stone such women. Now what do You say?" (John 8:2-5)

No Free Lunch

"There's no such thing as a free lunch," my high school biology teacher used to tell our sophomore class. Over time, I came to understand that the application of this expression is not limited to plates of peanut butter sandwiches and potato chips—everyone's got to pay, eventually, for what he or she gets.

If someone helps you out, you can count on the fact that someday he will be standing at your door, waiting to collect. No free lunches. It's orderly. Predictable. It makes sense. It's a system that we can all come to know and enforce. There's a price for everything.

It was a postcard-autumn day, and so I found myself walking through a wooded neighborhood not far from where I live. I treasured the gold of the late afternoon sun, looking to the right and the left to see how fall was coaxing color from trees and tugging to wrestle the first leaves from their high perches. My thoughts were ushered out from their private gallery, however, as I noticed a little boy on the edge of the road ahead, playing alone on the lawn in front of his house. As I approached, he left his own private game and came toward me.

"Would you like a bracelet?" he asked, tilting his head slightly to one side. My heart melted as I looked at the seven-year-old in front of me. In his hand was a priceless piece of art: two red maple leaves hanging from deep green blades of grass carefully looped and knotted together. A gift. An incredible gift from God's gallery through the hands of this child.

I reached out to take the present from the boy. To my surprise, my new friend took a step backwards. The autumn cherub became a small salesman in shorts and T-shirt. "They're only a quarter," he said, dangling the bracelet from his finger, his bony arm stretched out towards me. I then noticed that the finger offering the bracelet was attached to an open palm. "No free lunch," I remembered quietly.

No free lunch. We've become good at playing that game. We learn it in the school of experience. We learn it well and then teach it to our children. We then reinforce the lessons for one another. Satan grins and does some tutoring of his own on the subject. "Everyone's got to pay," becomes our regular recitation.

Nor is it a new idea. It is as old as the rocks and mountains. It is as ancient as the serpent. Long ago, after the harmony of the Garden had faded, the people of Yahweh came to live by this formula. They grew to acknowledge that there was a price to be paid. They knew well the Law, in which God Himself had told them: "Each is to die for his own sin" (Deuteronomy 24:16).

A perfect God could not casually ignore or wave away the sin of a rebellious people. Yahweh was grimly aware that the punishment for sin must be carried out in full force. Law, judgment, offering, and bloody sacrifice became a way of life for a people steeped in sin.

And so it was with a firm experience in the comfortable rigidity of the Law that a group of religious leaders came to Jesus one day. They didn't come alone. With them they brought a woman, whom they thrust out in front of them so that she might be exposed before the crowd. They were intent on making her private life public. Her sexual sin was to become the topic of a temple forum. From their perspective, this nuisance from Nazareth had planted Himself in the temple courts to teach. Let Him teach. Let Him struggle out of the trap they were about to lay for Him.

It is indeed a fascinating setting that John records for us in the eighth chapter of his gospel. Allow the scene to be painted in your mind as you read his words: "But Jesus went to the Mount of Olives. At dawn He appeared again in the temple courts, where all the people gathered around Him, and He sat down to teach them. The teachers of the law and the Pharisees brought in a woman caught in adultery. They made her stand before the group and said to Jesus, 'Teacher, this woman was caught in the act of adultery. In the Law Moses commanded us to stone such women. Now what do You say?' They were using this question as a trap, in order to have a basis for accusing Him" (John 8:1–6).

It was not the only time that they would try to trap Jesus. On another occasion the religious leaders sent their disciples to Jesus with words of flattery and a question about paying taxes (Matthew 22:15–22). Jesus saw through to their evil intent, boldly called them hypocrites, and asked them why they were trying to trap Him. He then countered their attack with such skill that they went away stripped of their weapons and strategy. At another time, they tried to work Him into a corner with queries about healing on the Sabbath (Matthew 12:9–14). Yet Jesus refused to ignore a man's need in order to keep the letter of the Law. He did not deny the waiting miracle but healed a withered hand, prompting the Pharisees to plot how they might kill Him.

Jesus was no stranger to controversy. And on this occasion, He was again put in the spotlight: "In the Law Moses commanded us to stone such women. Now what do You say?" (John 8:5).

What would Jesus do? Would He uphold the law of Moses and in the process act against His own Gospel of mercy, forgiveness, and freedom? Or would He side with an exposed adulteress and disregard the Law? Every ear waited for Jesus' answer. The trap was set. The bait stood with her left shoulder exposed, her chin resting on her chest. The Pharisees readied themselves to pounce. Jesus had already shown Himself to be—what they might call—characteristically soft on sinners. Yet the Pharisees knew that His decision would not be easy on this day. Someone would have to pay. And if this woman didn't, then Jesus would.

Leveling the Field

The stage has been set. The curtain's been drawn. Characters have found their places and recited their lines. I've followed the drama with mounting interest up until now. I'm all the way forward in my seat, clinging to my program, which I now find tightly rolled and wadded in my sweaty palm. Come on, Jesus. Say something!!

Take note of the divine response at the very climax of the unfolding drama: "But Jesus bent down and started to write on the ground with His finger" (John 8:6b).

What? Is that it? You've got to be kidding! What's with the scratching in the dirt? Is Jesus giving up? Is He going to roll over and play dead to avoid springing the trap? Has He lost His nerve? Have they manipulated Him into backing down?

I can see the Pharisees, first leaning forward, waiting for an answer ... then, with the silence increasing, some of them beginning to shift weight from one foot to the other ... then looking at each other and muttering ... and finally almost shouting their questions at Him, demanding to be answered. Yet Jesus was not afraid of the open jaws of their trap. He was not playing dead. Rather, He was deliberately and artfully acting to switch the bait of the trap which they themselves had set: "When they kept on questioning Him, He straightened up and said to them, 'If any one of you is without sin, let him be the first to throw a stone at her.' Again He stooped down and wrote on the ground" (John 8:7–8).

That's it. With incredible economy of words and emotions, Jesus has leveled the playing field. He has evened out the teams participating in this mismatched spectacle. He has refused to allow those in power to manipulate the situation at the expense of this woman. Jesus would not permit her to be paraded by the religious leaders for a theological game. Instead, He switched the focus from the woman to the sin. And Jesus acted to show them that the same sickness which infected this woman was present to just as great a degree in their own ailing hearts.

The following insight by author Robert Kinast may prove to be helpful in sorting through this situation:

> Jesus' antagonists did not ask an abstract question about a legal interpretation. They presented Him with a real person in a real situation. And Jesus identified with her. He no doubt saw in her and in the way she was being treated the terrible effects of sin. He knew what a grip it had on people. ...
>
> Out of this deep, compassionate bond He responded to their question as if to say: 'Sin is the human disordering of God's creation. Only God can finally put it right. If you think you're on God's level (as they accused Him of claiming for Himself), then do what you think God would do.' He went back to doodling, not to make light of the situation but to show His disregard for their misuse of it and to leave the dilemma with them.
>
> (From *If you Only Recognized God's Gift*, copyright © 1993 by Wm. B. Eerdmans Publishing Co. Used by permission.)

And so, having left the situation with them, they were forced to come to terms with their own sin. One by one, they grasped the impact of what Jesus had said. And one after another, they quietly wandered off, eventually leaving Jesus to stand alone with the woman. The story concludes quietly and thoughtfully:

"At this, those who heard began to go away one at a time, the older ones first, until only Jesus was left, with the woman still standing there. Jesus straightened up and asked her, 'Woman, where are they? Has no one condemned you?' 'No one, sir,' she said. 'Then neither do I condemn you,' Jesus declared. 'Go now and leave your life of sin' " (John 8: 9–11).

No Condemnation

This is truly a story of incredible power. In a world of "no free lunches," it demonstrates the radical grace that God freely poured out for us through Jesus Christ. Yet this account from John's gospel also provides a starting point for Christians as they struggle to interact with those around them who are trapped in immorality.

Building or maintaining a connection with someone caught up in sexual sin or other destructive behavior can pose an overwhelming challenge for Christians. Yet God commands us to bring Christ to a world swarming with sinners such as this. St. Paul writes in Philippians, "Do everything without complaining or arguing, so that you may become blameless and pure, children of God without fault in a crooked and depraved generation, in which you shine like stars in the universe as you hold out the word of life" (Philippians 2:14–16a).

We are not only to live pure and holy lives among such a generation, but we are also to *hold out the word of life* as we do so. We are to shine like stars so that others might see the true light of Christ. Who benefits if we keep the light to ourselves, gathering regularly to merely huddle around the glow? As God works in our lives, He thrusts our light out into the darkness of the world.

Because God provides fuel for the flame and direction for the beam through His holy Word, the Bible is both the object of a Christian's study and the agent through which the Holy Spirit moves us to action. Knowing that the devil does all he can to lead us away from God and His Word directs us all the more to the strength of the Scriptures. Martin Luther, in his preface to the Large Catechism, discusses the necessity of our daily reliance on the Word:

> **Why should I waste words? Time and paper would fail me if I were to recount all the blessings that flow from God's Word.**

The devil is called the master of a thousand arts. What, then, shall we call God's Word, which routs and destroys this master of a thousand arts with all his wiles and might? It must, indeed, be master of more than a hundred thousand arts. Shall we frivolously despise this might, blessing, power, and fruit—especially we who would be pastors and preachers? If so, we deserve not only to be refused food but also to be chased out by dogs and pelted with dung. Not only do we need God's Word daily as we need our daily bread; we also must use it daily against the daily, incessant attacks and ambushes of the devil with his thousand arts. ... O what mad, senseless fools we are! We must ever live and dwell in the midst of such mighty enemies as the devils, and yet we despise our weapons and armor, too lazy to give them a thought!

So it is to the Word that we turn once again as we ask God how He would have us shine for Him in the life of someone who is trapped in immorality. And it is the Word that points us once again to Jesus Christ. I would like to rely once again on Scripture as I highlight four things that Jesus did in dealing with the woman who was involved in a life of immorality.

First of all, Jesus saw this woman as a person, not as a category. He refused to consider this woman only as an "adulteress," although He fully recognized that she had been involved in adultery. He focused on the individual, rather than on the sin. In the same way, we need to remember that those trapped in immorality are *people* whom God created and whom He loves.

Second, Jesus leveled the playing field by reminding the teachers of the Law and the Pharisees of their own sinful condition. The woman was not the only one who required God's gracious hand in her life. And so Jesus dealt with *both* groups of lost people on that day. He demonstrated that *every* person in God's creation bears the bruises of the Fall. Even those who have put their faith in Christ continue to struggle with sin. We are reminded, "If we claim to be without sin, we deceive ourselves and the truth is not in us" (1 John 1:8).

In the book of Romans we see further evidence of this ongoing war that would consume the inner resources of every Christian. The apostle Paul sums up the battle in the closing verses of Romans 7: "So I find this law at work: When I want to do good, evil is right there with me. For in my inner being I delight in God's law; but I see another law at work in the members of my body, waging war against the law of my mind and making me a prisoner of the law of sin at work within my members. What a wretched man I am! Who will rescue me from this body of death?" (Romans 7:21–24).

Once we get honest about who we really are, the leveling of the playing field takes place quickly. We no longer are at liberty to see ourselves as judges wearing white gloves. In John 8, the Pharisees were in as much need of a Savior as the woman caught in the act of adultery. We are in a position to reach out to broken people with the Good News of Jesus only because God has already loved us in our brokenness.

Jesus announced a word of grace to the woman who was dragged before Him. She had been caught. Not only were the religious leaders pointing fingers at her, but God's holy Law stood as her accuser. She was well aware of her sin. But instead of upholding the just punishment for this transgression, Jesus released a flood of mercy that washed over this sinful woman. Imagine the release and gratitude that overwhelmed her as she heard those simple words from Jesus' lips: "Then neither do I condemn you" (John 8:11).

Many people with whom we come into contact are truly trapped in immorality. Regular abuse of substances and sex has led individuals to give up more and more of their freedom to make healthy decisions. Narcotics, alcohol, food, and money become objects of their addictions. The wanderings of such a hopeless life lead many to seek the help of professional counseling or 12-step groups. And there they are faced with the necessary first step to wholeness, and that is the admission that they are *powerless* against their addictions.

Yet isn't it true for all of us? St. Paul writes in Romans, "You see, at just the right time, *when we were still powerless*, Christ died for the ungodly. ... But God demonstrates His own love for us in this: While we were still sinners, Christ died for us" (Romans 5:6, 8, emphasis added).

Every one of us is waiting for the same unbelievable words that Jesus spoke to this broken woman. *Then neither do I condemn you.* God's grace breaks all established laws and attitudes. It goes against all that we have deemed to be fair. It crushes all reasonable religious thought. But this grace, in a world of "no free lunches," is made possible only because of the sacrifice of Jesus on a lonely hilltop, stretched out on the beam of a cross. *You see, at just the right time ... Christ died for the ungodly.*

The woman caught in adultery was not let off free. She was released without immediate payment for her sin, only because someone else was willing to pick up the tab. No, God could not turn His back on sin. There was a price to be paid. The punishment for sin was to be carried out in full, with scourge and nail and spear and thorn. But because of the offering of God's Son, the apostle Paul could later write these words of victory: "Therefore, there is now no condemnation for those who are in Christ Jesus" (Romans 8:1).

No condemnation. How many people outside the church do you know who are simply aching to hear these words? How many have become aware that their life is void of true meaning and long to be set free of the sin that possesses them? If you sense that the Holy Spirit is creating true sorrow for sin in the heart of someone you know who is caught up in immorality, then be bold to speak to him or her the words of Jesus: "Then neither do I condemn you." Demonstrate the acceptance to that individual that God has already shown to you. But quickly, then, bring him or her to the cross of Jesus where he or she might find true acceptance, not from you, but from God Himself! Then let God usher in the strength and courage for that person to leave the time-deepened ruts of sin.

In John's account of the woman caught in adultery, Jesus focused on the person and not the sin; He pointed out that every individual is equally dependent on God's mercy; He communicated a message of grace and healing. And finally, only after He had demonstrated the Father's heart by doing all of these things, did He instruct and encourage the woman to leave her sin behind.

Too often we would like to reverse the steps from John 8. We would like to share our own standards of religious behavior as our first contact with those who are caught up in immorality. We insist that they clean up their act so we might be free to welcome them into the church. We prod them with the Law and shout at them to somehow make themselves worthy of the Gospel. Rather than deal with the unpredictability of grace, we cling to the sure scaffolding of the Law.

Yet Jesus, in His encounter with the woman of this story, demonstrated a pure heart of love as His first move toward someone weighed down under the burden of the Law. And only after He had spoken to her a word of grace did He instruct her to leave her ways of sin. For without the strength that God provides through grace, it is a futile instruction indeed.

So once again we find ourselves talking about Jesus. Once again we return to Christ as the center of our conversations and our teaching. Our common encounters truly remain common until we point to the Jesus of the manger and the Christ of the cross. We therefore *must* talk about Christ in our common encounters with those trapped in immorality.

This emphasis on Christ cannot be stressed enough. For it is in the cross alone where the power lies. Oswald Chambers clearly maintains this understanding in his classic devotional, *My Utmost for His Highest:*

> Re-state to yourself what you believe, then do away with as much of it as possible, and get back to the bedrock of the Cross of Christ. ... The effect of the Cross is salvation, sanctification, healing, etc., but we are not to preach any of these, we are to preach Jesus Christ and Him crucified. The proclaiming of Jesus will do its own work. Concentrate on God's centre in your preaching, and though your crowd may apparently pay no attention, they can never be the same again. If I talk my own talk, it is of no more importance to you than your talk is to me; but if I talk the truth of God, you will meet it again and so will I."

Pray today that God would grant you the courage to "talk the truth of God" in your common encounters. And if you find yourself in such a conversation, whisper an inner prayer that the Spirit would involve you in a work of eternal consequence. *Though your crowd may apparently pay no attention, they can never be the same again.* May it be so, for Jesus' sake.

The Rest of the Story

So, what happened next? What happened to the woman who stood before her Redeemer on that day? Did the Pharisees seek her out later to deliver the punishment she deserved for her transgression? Did she leave Jesus' presence and tragically make her way back to the side of her lover? Or would she one day be found sobbing at the base of the cross, mourning the slow death of the one who had exchanged His life for hers? John doesn't tell us. And so we wonder.

It is sometimes frustrating to see only one side of the picture. Yet I tend to believe that she became a disciple of Jesus. For I have witnessed firsthand the healing and faith that is brought about by the gracious embrace of Jesus Christ.

We need never lose hope in our interactions with those who seem trapped in immoral behavior. For God is at work through our witness, and His desire is to free that person from the jaws of persistent sin and to bring him or her into His own family.

As you deal with those who are trapped in immorality or other spiritually destructive behaviors, carefully consider the words recorded in the fifty-fifth chapter of Isaiah:

> Seek the LORD while He may be found;
> call on Him while He is near.
> Let the wicked forsake his way
> and the evil man his thoughts.
> Let him turn to the LORD,
> and He will have mercy on him,
> and to our God, for He will freely pardon.
> "For My thoughts are not your thoughts,
> neither are your ways My ways," declares the LORD.
> "As the heavens are higher than the earth,
> so are My ways higher than your ways
> and My thoughts than your thoughts.
> As the rain and the snow
> come down from heaven,
> and do not return to it
> without watering the earth
> and making it bud and flourish …
> so is My word that goes out from My mouth:
> It will not return to Me empty,
> but will accomplish what I desire
> and achieve the purpose for which I sent it."
> (Isaiah 55:6–11)

These are God's words. Take them to heart. Hear His promise. Believe His offer for mercy. Acknowledge His power. Stand firm in His strength.

For Discussion

1. Look up Romans 6:23. How does this passage both support and shatter the concept of "no free lunch"? How is this apparent contradiction made possible? Support your answer with other references from Scripture.

2. After reading Leviticus 20:10, comment on what seems "fishy" about this woman being brought alone to judgment in this scenario. When the Pharisees brought the woman before Jesus in John 8, do you think they were really concerned for her as a person? How can we determine whether we have a sincere concern for those who are caught up in sin?

3. Whom do you know who is trapped in immorality? What kinds of opportunities have you had to reach out to that person? What parts of this chapter are helpful to you as you prepare for future opportunities?

4. "If any one of you is without sin, let him be the first to throw a stone at her," Jesus said. Why do you think that her accusers began to go away one at a time, *the older ones first?* What has been your own experience with the mastering of sin in your life? Why is this important to recall as you pray about witnessing to someone caught up in sin?

5. Jesus said to Nicodemus in John 3:17, "For God did not send His Son into the world to condemn the world, but to save the world through Him." Why is it so vital for us to center on Jesus in our conversations with those trapped in immorality? You may want to refer to the quote by Oswald Chambers as you continue to reflect on this question.

Session 5 Those in Affliction

As He went along, He saw a man blind from birth. (John 9:1)

If Only

The vision gradually grows clearer. Slowly the mists of the mind swirl around faint forms, eventually lifting to reveal images more distinct. Firm ground and black boots come first into view. Above the boots are tights, cape, muscled form. Hands boldly on hips, chin lifted high. Flushed cheeks, sparkling eyes. And emblazoned across rippling chest is the golden letter "E." No bird, no plane ... it's Super Evangelist.

Always ready to respond to the call, he bounds into neighborhoods, schools, and workplaces with agility and self-assurance. Spreading salvation far and wide, he flies through the air, flinging Gospel tracts and pocket New Testaments to those who stand gazing after his darting form. Quoting entire chapters from the Bible and confidently leading weeping sinners in prayer, he leads hundreds to faith with ease and elegance. At the end of each day he stands surrounded by singing angels, a smile spreading across his thin lips, realizing he has once again made a significant impact on a lost world.

The superhero picture shatters, however, as the alarm sounds. Angel voices are replaced by the intruding electronic signal. You hit the off button and roll over to glare at the digital readout of the clock. Morning routine. Lights on. The lingering steam and warmth of the bathroom summon you for a shower. As you rush to get dressed, the TV blares details of new fighting in Rwanda. But while you gulp your Lucky Charms, the dream lingers on. If only you were more outgoing, *then* you would be able to talk to that friend of yours who doesn't go to church. If only you knew your Bible better. If only you had a more convincing testimony. If only you had gone to a Christian school. If only.

Perhaps it's time to neatly fold the cape and put it away. For we can spend a lifetime explaining to ourselves why we weren't the right one for the job. But God's command is sure: "Therefore go and make disciples of all nations" (Matthew 28:19).

This charge is not just given to pastors and missionaries, but to every individual who carries the name of Christ in this world. Remember the words of 1 Peter: "Always be prepared to give an answer to everyone who asks you to give a reason for the hope that you have" (1 Peter 3:15).

These words cannot be explained away. These words are for you. In your family. At your university. Within your social circles. At your job.

I have come to accept that what is lacking many times in my own life is not the opportunity to witness but the willingness to witness. I, too, am liable to be heard uttering those words, "If only …" I must confess that I own neither boots nor cape. I bear no embroidered Es on my shirts. Yet I do have a deep love for Jesus. And sometimes I am surprised at how God patiently nudges me into situations where He gets the glory, despite my sluggish and self-directed nature.

It was a Sunday morning, and I was on my way to church. While driving through the sparse traffic, I glanced down at the dash. I noticed my truck's fuel gauge floating thinly on the line marked "empty." Corner gas station ahead on the right. I quickly looked at my watch and pulled the truck sharply into the station. Standing next to the pump, watching the whirl of the numbers marking my purchase, I thought back to the week that had just passed. It had been busy. Too busy. And as I thought through the previous days, I sadly realized that I had spent more time in my Daytimer than in the Bible. "I'm sorry, Lord," I whispered. I then prayed a heartfelt petition that God would replace my busyness with His presence, fill me with His Spirit, and draft me into His service throughout the coming week. As I consciously turned my life and will over to God once again, I began to sing softly the words from Psalm 51, which I had learned to rely on in times such as these:

> **"Create in me a clean heart, O God,
> and renew a right spirit within me.
> Cast me not away from Your presence,
> and take not Your Holy Spirit from me."**

So as other customers at the Mobil station washed their car windows and bought their Sunday papers, I prayed for renewal and

reports on the reactions to the first. John makes it clear that although the man's blindness had been taken away, he was not freed from affliction. For the newly healed man was accorded no more respect or dignity than when he used to sit at the side of the road. Those who had known him previously displayed an odd reaction to the healing: "His neighbors and those who had formerly seen him begging asked, 'Isn't this the same man who used to sit and beg?' Some claimed that he was. Others said, 'No, he only looks like him.' But he himself insisted, 'I am the man.' 'How then were your eyes opened?' they demanded" (John 9:8–10).

His neighbors had paid so little attention to him when he was blind that now they debated whether this was the same man. But things were different now. They were used to seeing him sitting; now he was standing before them. They had grown accustomed to hearing his voice; now they looked into his face. He used to be an ignored segment of their community; now he had a story that had to be reckoned with.

They demanded that he explain how his eyes had been opened. All the poor man could do was tell them about Jesus. They took him to the Pharisees, and there, too, he gave testimony to Jesus. His witness was personal and powerful: "One thing I do know. I was blind but now I see" (John 9:25).

They continued to interrogate him, not willing to accept the obvious conclusions about the one who had healed him. Eventually the man who had been blind told them what he thought about Jesus: "Nobody has ever heard of opening the eyes of a man born blind. If this man were not from God, He could do nothing" (John 9:32–33).

This was the last thing the Pharisees wanted to hear: "To this they replied, 'You were steeped in sin at birth; how dare you lecture us!' And they threw him out" (John 9:34).

Ridiculed and rejected, he left their presence. Imagine his confusion as he slowly wandered home. Perhaps he had been tricked by nothing more than a series of illusions: the idea that someone cared about him ... a freshly-painted picture of a productive future ... the hope that God was good ... Maybe a blind beggar was merely being taunted by a colorful vision that life could be different from what he had always pictured.

But then, at what could have been his darkest hour, in walks Jesus. Having heard that the they threw him out, the Healer came and found the man who was about to undergo his second surgery. The restoration of sight had taken place. The miracle of faith was about to be given: "When He found him, He [Jesus] said, 'Do you believe in the Son of Man?' 'Who is He, sir?' the man asked. 'Tell me so that I may believe in Him.' Jesus said, 'You have now seen Him; in fact, He is the one speaking with you.' Then the man said, 'Lord, I believe,' and he worshiped Him" (John 9:35b–38).

And with those surprisingly ordinary words, another individual has stepped across the threshold into the household of God. Another common conversation has ended in salvation. Once more, an encounter with Jesus has led to a gift which can only be bought and wrapped by God Himself.

God has strangely chosen, however, to place this precious gift in the hands of clumsy couriers. He has embraced the foolishness of relying on us to carry out the delivery of this costly present. Through His Spirit and our willing witness, God has oddly planned to bring eternal life to those who would accept the gift.

As you go about the days ahead, ask God to give you true empathy for those who walk through the dark days of affliction. Pray that God would alarm you at the thought of others enduring the night of eternal separation from their Creator. Ask Him to make you a faithful witness to Jesus Christ, the light of the world.

And as you endure afflictions of your own, hold fast to the words of Paul as he writes to the Philippians:

> But whatever was to my profit I now consider loss for the sake of Christ. What is more, I consider everything a loss compared to the surpassing greatness of knowing Christ Jesus my Lord, for whose sake I have lost all things. I consider them rubbish, that I may gain Christ and be found in Him, not having a righteousness of my own that comes from the law, but that which is through faith in Christ—the righteousness that comes from God and is by faith. I want to know Christ and the power of His resurrection and the fellowship of sharing in His sufferings, becoming like Him in His death, and so, somehow, to attain to the resurrection from the dead. (3:7-11)

May God use your afflictions to focus your life on what truly matters. And may He instill in you an urgency to bring light to those who sit in darkness.

For Discussion

1. Whom do you know who comes the closest to fitting the description of "Super Evangelist"? Why is it such a dangerous idea to leave the work of Christian outreach to the Super Evangelists, with the rationalization that they are the most qualified for the job?

2. Think back to the story of Rona. Have you ever prayed for God to use you and then been surprised when He has? Do you know someone who knows affliction but doesn't know Christ? What do the words from Matthew 5:14–16 suggest about the kind of role you might play in that person's life?

3. "There will always be more questions than answers." What is the danger in trying to answer every question that someone in affliction might pose for us? What comfort do you find in the hope that God holds out for us in 1 Corinthians 13:12?

4. "It is only when we are uncomfortable that we learn lessons that matter." Do you agree with this statement? Why or why not? How does this apply to your work of reaching out with the Gospel to those who are in affliction?

Session 6
The Grieving

O n His arrival, Jesus found that Lazarus had already been in the tomb for four days. Bethany was less than two miles from Jerusalem, and many Jews had come to Martha and Mary to comfort them in the loss of their brother. When Martha heard that Jesus was coming, she went out to meet Him. (John 11:17–20)

Death Allowed

I wonder what emotions must have tugged at Jesus' heart when He heard that His dear friend Lazarus was sick. Sorrow? Concern? Alarm? The brief message He received from Mary and Martha hints at how deeply He cared for this family: "Lord, the one You love is sick" (John 11:3).

The expectation was that He would come immediately. Of course He would come. He had to come. How could He cure the clamoring masses yet ignore the call of one who brought Him joy?

Martha, Mary, and Lazarus had opened their home to Jesus. They had shared many laughter-filled evenings with Him around their small table. Theirs was a bond that others could only envy. Jesus was sure to give first priority to this precious friendship. Yet it was apparently not to be: "When He heard that Lazarus was sick, He stayed where He was two more days" (John 11:6).

He stayed away knowing that Lazarus would die. Unbelievable. Unnatural. An incredible thing. To have the power but not use it—was that ethical? Was it moral? At the very least, was it *loving?* The Jews who mourned with Mary and Martha wagged their heads and tongues: "Could not He who opened the eyes of the blind man have kept this man from dying?" (John 11:37).

How could He have refused the need? How could one who claimed to be Life allow death to claim another victim, idly looking on while it stalked a close friend? Mary and Martha had identical responses to Jesus' baffling lack of concern for their family: "Lord, if You had been here, my brother would not have died" (John 11:21, 32).

Death had ignored their unique relationship with Jesus, claiming the brother they loved.

Death. We know it as more than just a first-century phenomenon. Twenty centuries later, it continues to walk into lives without warning or welcome. It ignores the fences around our homes and slips past our security systems. It laughs at deadbolts and doors. It disregards muffled cries and welcomes furrowed brows. It looks about with taunting eyes and quickly snatches up the best-loved son, closest friend, dearest brother. And those left behind console one another with fading memories of the one who was taken.

The people of our age are all too familiar with such sentiments. Our own tears flow as death has its way with us as well. The loss of one we love displays the awful difference between what might be and what is.

How could God create us for life and then allow our shallow breath to leave us so quickly? We somberly observe the fleeting nature of life along with the Psalmist:

> You sweep men away in the sleep of death;
> they are like the new grass of the morning—
> though in the morning it springs up new,
> by evening it is dry and withered. ...
> The length of our days is seventy years—
> or eighty, if we have the strength;
> yet their span is but trouble and sorrow,
> for they quickly pass, and we fly away. (Psalm 90:5-6, 10)

Reluctant to acknowledge the hand of death, we resist the reality of loss. We kick and struggle against its unwelcome intrusion into our well-planned lives. Yet it persists in its unrelenting penetration, ignoring the streak of tears on our twisted faces.

Confusion and frustration are apparent in our normally calm voices. Like the sisters who counted on the intervening hand of God, we utter the words, "Lord, if only You had been here." We may come to the point where we acknowledge His power but question His plan. We might submit to His will; yet we wonder at His ways. We gulp the wine of grief, which gives us the courage to interrogate the Infinite. We plead for answers. Yet our sin-blurred eyes are unable to focus on the picture which God Himself has sketched, a scene which holds a triumphant Christ at the center of its frame.

It is this picture which Jesus has in mind as He tells His disciples, "Lazarus is dead, and for your sake I am glad I was not there, so that you may believe" (John 11:14).

Death has had its own way—for now. Yet God has permitted death, so that the fullness of life might be displayed.

With Those Who Grieve

A friend of mine caught up with me in our office one morning in early December. As we talked, we perched ourselves on either side of the copy machine, waiting for the warm sheets of paper to slide out into the tray. More was on her mind than making copies, however. Eventually the conversation turned to what she really wanted to discuss. "Will you pray for my friend Jan?" she asked me earnestly. "Her mother is dying."

I assured her that I would keep Jan in my prayers. My friend displayed her missionary heart as she continued: "I've been trying to get Jan to come to church with me, but she's always got a reason why she can't make it. I'm real concerned for her. Pray that God would use this situation to bring her back to church."

It was about a week later that Jan's mother was given relief from her sickness. Jan and her husband welcomed the relief but still mourned the loss. Throughout that time of grief, however, God used my friend as a confident witness of the Gospel in their lives. She stood by Jan during that time, sharing the pain of those difficult days.

Shortly before Christmas my friend's eyes sparkled with the good news: "Jan came to church with me last Sunday! She thanked me for inviting her. I think she's going to come back next week and bring her husband with her!" My friend had seen the open door that this time of grief provided. She had taken advantage of it by sharing her own love and the love of Jesus for that family. She had used a time of grieving to share her faith and hope in God.

It is inevitable that each of us crosses paths with grief. Not every day will hold wispy clouds and bright sunshine. Every one of us will experience the storms of death and mourning in the lives of those we know, as well as in our own lives.

Death is more than the bluster of wind and the pelt of hail. Death is also opportunity. For those who *die* in Jesus, it is an open door into eternal life ("Today you will be with Me in paradise" [Luke 23:43]. For those who *live* in Jesus, the death of a loved one is an occasion to "proclaim the mystery of Christ" (Colossians 4:3).

It is inevitable that we will eventually sit with our arm around one who has lost a brother or grandfather, sister or wife, acquaintance or companion. And for those of us who know Christ, this situation brings not only grief, but also opportunity. Like the death of Martha and Mary's brother, this can be "for God's glory so that God's Son may be glorified through it" (John 11:4). As we answer the call of those who have lost loved ones, we can follow the example of Jesus in John 11.

Like Jesus, we can come to the side of those who have experienced loss. We offer ourselves freely with the same goal that Jesus stated: "that God's Son may be glorified." And through our ready feet and tongues, we pray that the grieving would be comforted not only by us, but also by the Comforter. Through our own embrace, we pray that they might be brought to the open arms of a loving God.

As we consider our openings to witness to the grieving, we dare not disregard the difficult questions brought on by death. Frustration and anger may be a part of the mourner's experience:

- "If there is a God, why did He allow this to happen?"
- "I thought God was supposed to be loving."
- "Where has God been through the most difficult days of my life?"
- "I could never trust in a God who would take away the one who meant the most to me."

In effect, they are all variations of the same theme: "Lord, if You had been here ..." Jesus was able to deal with Martha and Mary's concerns, however, because He knew the heart of His Father toward them and toward their brother, Lazarus. Jesus saw the bigger picture that they could not entirely take in. He was aware that Lazarus' grave was soon to be empty. More important, Jesus knew that His own death and resurrection would affect the brother who now lay in the grave: "For as in Adam all die, so in Christ will all be made alive" (1 Corinthians 15:22).

As we reach the side of unbelievers who grieve, God is able to keep us from drowning in the swirling waters of their doubt and despair. He will equip us to provide certain comfort, because He has shared with us His heart toward them and toward us. The Scriptures assure us that although sin and disease and death have set up their tyrannous rule in our world, their regime is not under the approval of the King. And though God allows their rebel ways for a time, their reign is limited. God loves His world and desires to be in relationship with each of its inhabitants.

We may confidently describe a loving God to those who mourn: "For God so loved the *world* ..." (John 3:16, emphasis added). Jesus has "come so that they may have life, and have it to the full" (John 10:10). And perhaps this death was allowed "so that you may believe" (John 11:15). God may use *any* situation to His glory, for He "wants all ... to be saved and to come to the knowledge of the truth" (1 Timothy 2:4).

Although we may not be able to answer each troubling question of the bereaved, we must dare to tell them the truth about God. Although we will be faced with problems for which we do not have solutions, we can assure them of what we do know: God's original intentions of good for this world and His tenacious insistence on bringing it right again through Jesus Christ.

Remember Paul's words to Timothy as he tirelessly tells again of God's plan through His Son: "For there is one God and one mediator between God and men, the man Christ Jesus, who gave Himself as a ransom for all" (1 Timothy 2:5–6).

Jesus has paid the price. He has offered up Himself. He has changed the relationship between God and man. And Paul has accepted his own calling to share the message, so that others might believe: "And for this purpose I was appointed a herald and an apostle ... and a teacher of the true faith to the Gentiles" (1 Timothy 2:7).

Like Paul, we have been commissioned as messengers of this truth. God has sent us, also, "to the Gentiles"—to those who are outside the community of faith. Jesus came so that we might have life. And it is our privilege to share the Life with the living.

Life for the Living

So with life on His mind, up the road toward the home of Martha and Mary walks God-in-the-flesh. Trudging behind Him are His closest followers, certain that they are making their way toward Bethany and nearby Jerusalem to witness the execution of their Master and Teacher at the hands of the people there. They have resigned themselves to die along with Jesus. Yet the conversation which is to soon take place contradicts all assumptions about life and death.

Martha meets Jesus out on the road. "Lord, if You had been here" are her first words. Her mind is a mix of grief and confusion. Lazarus is gone, and the one who could have prevented it stands before her. Her doubts are stirred with faith, however, and she continues, "But I know that even now God will give You whatever You ask" (John 11:22).

Martha's heart seems to anticipate a miracle. Jesus' answer, however, seems to be more of a funeral-home response. "Your brother will rise again," He tells her. His words sound distant. To us, His statement may appear to be a dead-end response. Yet in Jesus' strategy, these words are only the base of a conversation which has salvation as its peak.

Martha continues the dialog: "I know he will rise again in the resurrection at the last day" (John 11:24).

Her words are not empty. Nor are they to be taken for granted. In a day when many religious leaders didn't believe in any type of resurrection, her statement reflects the hope she had likely gained from Jesus Himself. He had taught her well. She had taken hold of this truth.

Up to this point, the dialog between Jesus and Martha has been commonplace. Facts have been shared. Truth has been affirmed. Consoling words have been spoken. Yet this ordinary conversation is about to take a turn. Jesus is ready to reveal a claim which shakes the foundations of death and hell. He is about to knock the mortuary doors off of their hinges: "I am the resurrection and the life. He who believes in Me will live, even though he dies; and whoever lives and believes in Me will never die" (John 11:25–26).

The friend of Lazarus has moved Martha from a general belief in the resurrection to a specific belief in Himself. "I AM the resurrection," He claims. "I AM the life," He asserts. He holds out faith in Himself as the key which turns the lock in the door to life.

As we comfort those who grieve, we find ourselves one more time telling about Jesus. Centering our conversation on Christ forces us to sidestep all the hopeless ideas that our culture hangs on to when it considers death.

Notice that Jesus doesn't ask Martha to consider nebulous concepts of an "afterlife." He holds out no images of the dead becoming angels who tuck their loved ones into bed at night. No tunnels of light. No emotional eulogies filled with half-truths about the goodness of the deceased. But an unwavering focus on Himself. Life forever to those who believe in Jesus. JESUS—the target toward which our arrow flies as we comfort those who grieve.

Without Christ we have no hope, no salvation, no assurance. St. Paul shared this truth with the church in Corinth: "If Christ has not been raised, your faith is futile; you are still in your sins" (1 Corinthians 15:17).

What kind of confidence could we possibly have at the point of death without Jesus? None—unless we are counting on somehow appearing spotless through our own good works before God. But the apostle goes on to say: "But Christ has indeed been raised from the dead, the firstfruits of those who have fallen asleep. ... Thanks be to God! He gives us the victory through our Lord Jesus Christ" (1 Corinthians 15:20, 57).

Death swallowed up in victory. The sting of death soothed through the blood of Jesus. And all of this through the work of the God-man, Jesus Christ. It is doubtful that more beautiful words can be found than those of Martin Luther, as he describes Christ's triumph over death and the devil:

> If we have the Son of God, who faces death and opposes the devil on our behalf, on our side, let the devil rage as he will. If the Son of God died for me, let death consume and devour me; for he will surely have to return and restore me, and I will stand my ground against him. Christ died; death devoured the Son of God; ... and since both God and man in one indivisible Person entered into the belly of death and the devil, death ate a morsel that ripped his stomach open.
>
> It was the counsel of God the Father from eternity to destroy death, ruin the kingdom of the devil, and give the devil a little pill which he would gleefully devour, but which would create a great rumpus in his belly and in the world. Now the Lord wants to say: "... Is it a miracle that I, the Son of man and the Son of God in one Person, am sacrificed and enter the jaws of death and the devil? But I shall not remain there. Not only will I come forth again, but I will also rip open death's belly; for the poison is too potent, and death itself must die." (*Luther's Works* 22:355)

This truth, described by Luther with so much passion, is what every Christian can be certain of. This reality is also what Jesus has in mind as He speaks tenderly with Martha in John 11. He Himself will soon offer up His life to accomplish the death of Death. He has assured her that HE is the resurrection and the life. Yet the next words that Jesus speaks to her make up the crucial question which separate salvation from condemnation, life from death, and heaven from hell. His words of life call for a response from His listener: "Do you believe this?" (John 11:26b).

All of heaven waits in expectation. Yet Martha's answer is immediate and faith-filled: " 'Yes, Lord,' she told Him, 'I believe that You are the Christ, the Son of God, who was to come into the world' " (John 11:27).

Her words express much more than reliance on a prophet. They run deeper than simple gratitude toward one who has healed. They surpass common respect for a gifted teacher. They are more than an awe-filled response to seeing miracles performed. Her confession brings life. It is Spirit-prompted and Christ-centered. It ushers one more individual into the presence of God Almighty.

"Yes, I believe." We long to hear those same words spoken from the lips of those to whom we witness. It is in our prayers that this kind of sure faith in Jesus would be granted to them, as well.

We cannot bring the dead to life. But through our steady care and sure words, God's Spirit can lead the living to life.

The Thing that Matters

I write these words on an evening flight from Phoenix to St. Louis. Below me, the peaks and canyons of Arizona lose their grand dimensions and melt into a flat dark mat. Only the winking lights of scattered towns beg silently to be noticed. At 37,000 feet, I sense that I am far removed from that distant time and place of Martha, Mary, and Lazarus. Could their world have anything to offer mine?

I wonder. And yet I have just concluded an out-of-the-ordinary conversation with the person who shares a plastic armrest with me. We have spent the last hour talking about the faith we share in Jesus of Nazareth. Once again, this conversation was brought about by God's timing, not by my keen spiritual awareness. The man next to me simply asked, "So, are you a believer?" His question was prompted by the Christian message on my T-shirt. As a result of this straightforward question, God brought two Christians together on an airplane to encourage one another in the faith.

As we talked, however, it wasn't long before the anonymous college student sitting next to us laid aside his crossword puzzle to hear what we were saying. Pretty soon, he was throwing in questions and comments of his own. God's little party was just gaining momentum. For not long after that, I found myself talking to the man's teenage son and daughter about getting involved in our youth group. And as I now sit collecting my thoughts, I am taken back that God has just led me into another encounter which may carry its weight into eternity.

I am humbly aware that just as Jesus walked into the world of Martha and Mary, He continues to walk into mine. I am confident that as Jesus called Lazarus forth from the tomb, so will He call me out from my grave with a shout and the crack of a trumpet blast. I know that I will stand before God's throne and sing out the words "Worthy is the Lamb who was slain!" along with Lazarus and his sisters. And I pray that I shall look around while standing in the presence of my Savior and see those thankful faces which I once saw on those oh-so-ordinary days—days when I was pumping gas or making copies or riding on an airplane.

At this moment, high above the earth, temporarily removed from the world which usually holds me, I realize that there's one thing which really matters. Only one thing …

> **Whom have I in heaven but You?**
> **And earth has nothing I desire besides You.**
> **My flesh and heart may fail,**
> **but God is the strength of my heart**
> **and my portion forever. …**
> **As for me, it is good to be near God.**
> **I have made the Sovereign Lord my refuge;**
> *I will tell of all Your deeds.*
> **(Psalm 73:25–26, 28, emphasis added)**

For Discussion

1. Have you ever been surprised or taken back to see that God has allowed the death of a certain individual? What

does Jesus state as His purpose for allowing the death of Lazarus? Tell of an incident where the death of an individual caused a situation leading to God's glory?

2. In what ways can the death of a loved one be a time of extreme hopelessness? How can it turn out to be one of the most hope-filled times that a Christian will ever know? How might you share this hope with those who are grieving?

3. "Death is opportunity," the author states. In what ways? What are some specific things you might do to help a grieving friend find sure footing on the rock of Jesus Christ?

4. Study Romans 8:31–39. What kind of assurance does God give to Christians through this passage? Is it possible to hold a belief in the resurrection without having belief in Jesus? Why is it necessary to link these two?

5. Fred Craddock, in *Preaching* (Nashville: Abingdon Press, 1985), makes the following comments on Jesus' use of common conversations throughout the gospel of John: "In each case, what begins as a private conversation grad-

ually enlarges to address the reader and all who will hear the witness of faith. Whatever may be the topic as the conversation begins, the ending is always a revelation of God giving life eternal to those who believe."

What specific examples of the Craddock's words can you recall from the gospel of John? How does God promise to bless your encounters?